ABOUT THE AUTH

Chris Gibson has been at the forefront of the global franchise industry for over ten years. There isn't anything he doesn't know about operating a successful franchise business or what someone thinking about buying a franchise should consider. Working with some of the best known franchise concepts as a CEO, Franchise Director and Vice President, more recently he set up Franology, "The Science of Franchising", a consulting business that works with the client not only on the strategic planning and pre-launch project but also on developing the business during the post-launch phase to ensure maximum benefit for the client. The ongoing relationship with clients, coupled with Franology's commitment to developing a client's successful business until eventual exit, has proved a highly cost-effective way to develop a franchise for clients.

A regular contributor to the industry press, he has appeared on television and is an accomplished orator, speaking regularly at conventions, lectures and on radio.

Follow Chris Gibson on Twitter @ChrisGAuthor
Facebook - Chris Gibson Author Page

"I have known Chris for many years and this book contains many very practical tips for franchisees and franchisors; tips gained from firsthand experience."

Mark Scott
Director Franchise Development Nat West/RBS Franchise Team

"Chris Gibson and his business Franology made it possible to Franchise my business, Happy Steps. I had an idea, but with step by step help it became a reality. Chris made the business easy to understand and was always there to help or give extra support when needed. I read his first book and found it interesting and helpful. Not only for me as a franchisor but for my perspective franchisees."

Debbie Harding, Founder Happy Steps

"Chris Gibson took me under his wing and helped grow my Franchise operation. Chris helped me with the process involved in attracting a franchisee, closing a sale and how to handle their expectations. Chris was always on hand to give me great advice. Chris Gibson certainly helped me with my Franchise model and took it from an idea to a great business for others to use."

Tony Charles, Managing Director at Foundation Football

For my wonderful gorgeous daughter Allie, who has given me so much love and laughter and put up with me being away from home over the years, often working in a foreign country for long periods.

For Helen, bringing up our daughter, single handed at times, while I earned us a crust. Perhaps one day you will understand the sacrifice was made with best intentions, not for the worst of outcomes.

Vitualamen in vita adveho procul a pretium
(*Sacrifices in life come at a price*)

Franchising Exposed
A Definitive Guide for Anyone Looking to Buy a Franchise or Develop a Franchised Concept

Chris Gibson

alliebooks

Published by alliebooks.co.uk

A division of Franology Limited – The Science of Franchising

Franchising Exposed

A Definitive Guide for Anyone Looking to Buy a Franchise
or Develop a Franchised Concept
By Chris Gibson

Published by:
alliebooks.co.uk
A Division of Franology Limited
158 Hermon Hill
South Woodford
London
E18 1QH

ISBN 978-0-9567618-0-4
eBook Versions available in ePub (8-0) and Mobi (9-7)
Copyright © 2010 Chris Gibson (Second Imprint 2013)
Orders@alliebooks.co.uk
www.alliebooks.co.uk

Unattributed quotations are by Chris Gibson

British Library Cataloguing in Publication Data
A catalogue record for this book is available from the British Library

Cover photography and design by I Heart Studios (www.iheartstudios.com)
Edited by Rushmore University Editing Services (www.rushmore.edu)

This book is intended as a reference volume only, not as a definitive business manual. The information given here is designed to help you make informed decisions about your business options.

Mention of specific companies, organisations, individuals or authorities in this book does not imply endorsement by the author or publisher, nor does mention of specific companies, organisations, individuals or authorities in the book imply that they endorse the book.

Addresses and websites given in this book were correct at the time of going to press.

alliebooks

Contents

Part One

So You Want to be a Franchisee

1

Once Upon A Time
A History of Franchising

Where it all started

Franchising is born – a potted history of franchising

It's a brilliant concept – get someone else to buy your idea, then charge him an ongoing share of the profits for making it work!

Once you understand the franchising concept, and how it evolved, you'll understand what is so good about franchising.

On the other hand, if you want to get straight into the meat of the book, move on to Chapter Two!

The most logical association with the modern day franchising concept is America, but there are references to a form of franchising throughout history.

Many tyrannical warlords in ancient China granted trade routes. The first chain stores actually appeared around 200BC when a businessman called Lo Kass set up a number of shops in his province, then used local partners to establish a bigger network of stores all selling the same products. This seems to fit the basic franchise model.

1066 – Not Quite; The emergence of franchising

The forerunner to the word *franchise* is probably the Old French word *franc*, which means "granting legal immunity" but could now be defined as protecting a person's right to do something.

In medieval Europe, landowners would grant rights to a variety of activities, such as hunting or brewing of ale. This was a win-win solution: the peasants used their rights to earn a living, and the landowner lived in style on his share of the profits. Sounds really good to me!

The aristocracy certainly had a keen eye for a business opportunity: the rich received a slice of the tolls charged on the roads, a share of produce or a share of the livestock, and even free horseshoes from the blacksmith who could also turn his hand to making swords as a bladesmith to pay for his agreement. In short, the nobles fed and equipped their men and servants without using their growing stockpile of gold. Lords became even richer.

In return, "men at arms" protected the land as part of the arrangement and eventually the agreement became a little more formal. Paper licences were as much use as chocolate teapots to the semi-literate peasants, so the agreements were later enacted into laws and bylaws to protect all the royal subjects.

Religion Plays its Part

The Catholic Church played its part as well, with the first form of territory planning that was certainly copied later by business people.

These territories fell under the direct control of local men of the cloth who granted papal rights in return for vast sums of money that they filtered back to Rome.

A Whole New World

In the rapidly developing new world, exclusive rights to trade routes, such as the Cape of Good Hope, were granted by royal charter.

More followed and in 1607 the London Company received the Charter for Virginia until the British Crown withdrew the Charter for mismanagement in 1624. Was this the first termination of an agreement?

It was the Second Industrial Revolution during the mid-1800s when German brewers granted licences or franchises to taverns, thereby increasing production and turnover and taking a slice of the taverns' income. Genius!

In 1851 the Singer Sewing Machine Company granted its first licence to distributors of its sewing machines. Some may say that this was not unique but Singer was the first company to have a written franchise contract with these distributors.

Frederick Henry Harvey opened the first of many restaurants in 1876 on the Topeka and Santa Fe line. The railroad company liked the concept and Harvey eventually opened one every hundred miles along the 12,000 mile route. Harvey saw the importance of control and instigated field visits and quality control, which are the basis of modern franchisor control systems.

A New Century

Transport changed everything as Americans started to move around in new automobiles from state to state. Branding became important, with the transient population looking for products they could identify with.

To cater for this explosion of brand awareness, companies like Coca Cola granted licences to other bottling plants that in turn supplied the famous drink locally.

Louis Liggett had a fabulous idea to expand his drug store chain in 1902. He charged $4000 to existing pharmacies to join the Rexall chain, invested the fees charged wisely and created a cooperative that supplied cheaper products to the licensees, so they benefitted financially. It went pretty well and at its height Rexall had 11,000 stores in the US, compared to 12,000 McDonald's today. That's quite a few!

Western Auto went the other way in 1909 and recruited people without any experience as car salesmen; this was the forerunner of modern day franchises, with support given in return for a royalty fee.

Regarded then as an innovative approach, this is the way most franchise companies operate today.

The Roaring Twenties and Through the Depression

Sherman and J Willard Marriott bought a franchise from the root beer giant A&W in the early 1920s. A&W used carhops on roller skates to generate more sales and the Marriott brothers added food to the menu, which worked even better. Their success is evident today with a certain hotel group that is rather large.

Howard Dearing Johnson tested the franchise concept in another market when he acquired a pharmacy in Massachusetts and began to sell three flavours of ice cream, as well as food, to supplement his drug sales. After success he awarded his first franchise in 1935 and the number of orange-roofed stores expanded dramatically. Another hotel giant we recognise today.

Hi Honey I'm Home

World War II came to an end, soldiers returned home and over the next decade people started to look for independence in their working life, owning their own business.

Fast food franchising really took off. Kentucky Fried Chicken, Burger King, Dunkin Donuts and McDonald's opened in the 1950s and franchised operations opened in far greater numbers than company owned operations, which meant rapid brand expansion.

KFC got it absolutely right with quality and a separate image of the founder. Harland Saunders was a real person; he spent years cooking chicken and adopted the white suit and string tie as an image after he was given the title of Kentucky Colonel, hence Colonel Saunders. The reason he looked so old was because he started franchising aged 62 in 1952. It's never too late!

Success started a trend of copycat franchises which the big names tried to stop on numerous occasions through all legal means available. This was humorously depicted in the John Landis film "Coming to America", starring Eddie Murphy, when the subplot revolved around McDowell's, a fast food restaurant serving the Big Mick, a burger with two beef patties, special sauce, lettuce, cheese and onions on buns with no seeds, compared to McDonald's Big Mac that used sesame seeded buns.

McDowell's had the Golden Arcs whereas McDonald's had the Golden Arches. Light-hearted but so true of many "me too" franchises around today. McDonald's obviously agreed to the comparison made by Landis, who made sure that McDowell's portrayed similar standards to McDonald's in the film.

Britain sits up and takes note – What a splendid idea

The Americans redesigned the franchise concept during the first half of the 20th Century. After making many mistakes, a hybrid version of a business format franchise evolved, and it looked good.

One of the first of the new style franchises in the UK was set up when J Lyons & Co acquired the rights to Wimpy from the US founder, Eddie Gold, in 1955.

Lyons Maid and Mr Softee offered licences to their first franchisees in the 1950s.

Gradually, over the next ten years, more concepts were either brought into the UK from overseas or new concepts were developed and marketed as franchise opportunities. Names like DynoRod, KFC, and Prontaprint emerged as national brands in the UK.

The poor economy of the 1970s contributed to the stagnation of franchising until interest rates came down and growth returned.

The franchise industry was keen to develop a code of ethics to ensure controlled regulation and in 1977 the British Franchise Association (bfa) was formed by some of the pioneers in UK franchising with DynoRod, Service Master, KFC, Wimpy, Holiday Inns, and Prontaprint all contributing to the birth of the association.

Recent history for franchising in the UK shows the success of the industry. Many High Street names have a link to franchising; The Body Shop, Tie Rack, McDonald's, Hertz, Domino's Pizza, Cartridge World, Snap On Tools, Subway, Bargain Booze – the list goes on and is certainly impressive compared to the early days of franchising in the UK.

They all lived happily ever after –The future's bright, the future is franchising!

I could stop here and say everything is wonderful in franchising, but that would be unprofessional.

Franchising is not for everyone; some think it is a way of buying a job, with success a mere formality. Not everyone can make it happen, but for those who follow the system and work hard, a good concept can provide a great business.

Nat West carries out a survey every year with the bfa, and the facts speak for themselves: over 85% of franchise businesses are still operating after five years compared to 20% for stand-alone businesses. Less than 3% of franchises suffer financial failure and over 400,000 people are employed in UK franchising, which had an annual turnover of nearly £13bn at the last count.

The future is bright and the wealth creation and thus asset security over the last twenty years through property prices has helped with the acceptance from the major banks that franchising is a lower risk lend than a non-proven business venture.

More companies today are considering launching their business as a new franchise, which is why section two of this book is dedicated to the operational side of running a franchise company. Recruiting new franchisees to gain a larger market share is a low risk strategy avoiding huge capital investment in premises and employees. If a franchise business develops in a proper manner then both franchisee and franchisor should benefit.

2

Now Which One Will I Choose?

What franchise is right for you?

That all important decision– it's not easy!

First decision – Why franchising instead of setting up my own new business?

It is fair to assume, because you are reading a book on franchising, that you are considering buying a franchise or starting a business on your own. It therefore makes sense to consider franchising versus going it alone before you make your final decision.

To help you make an informed decision first consider what is involved in starting your own business. Perhaps you have a business idea, or dream of working for yourself in a similar role to your current or previous working life. Thousands of businesses start trading every year, with the proprietors muddling through the various tasks required at their own pace. During the set-up they will encounter suppliers that refuse credit terms for purchases, costs for design and website development, and make a few mistakes as they strive to build a profitable business.

According to statistics collated by The Warwick Business School, only 20% will survive five years' trading; for various reasons, 80% will go out of business, through choice or necessity. Odds of 1:5 is a risky investment, in my opinion. Nat West and the bfa carry out a regular survey for the franchise community, which shows only 2.1% of franchise businesses fail, due to financial reasons, every year. If you extrapolate this rate then around 90% of franchised businesses continue to trade past five years: the increased chances of success and reduced risk are fairly clear.

For more information on the Nat West Survey visit www. natwest.com/business/services/market-expertise/franchising. ashx

Buying a franchise means an initial investment and ongoing licence fees or royalties, but with a blueprint already drafted and many set-up costs eliminated, the comparative cost is far less than the figure in isolation shows.

I mentioned in Chapter One that people can't just buy a job when buying a franchise and expect success as a mere formality. You have to work hard and follow the programme and keep doing the right things every day.

One question that I get asked regularly is "why would I buy a franchise, pay all that money and earn less in the first year compared to staying employed?" In response let me present franchising, as I would to answer this question if I were talking to you in person.

Somebody buys a franchise for £25,000, follows the programme and in their first year turn over £50,000 with a margin of 50%, so they make a gross profit of £25,000, less operating costs of £10,000, so they earned £15,000 compared to a job paying £25,000. Now that may seem bad, but in the second year they turn over £90,000, making a gross profit of £45,000 less the same operating costs of £10,000 so make £35,000, which is better than the £25,000 salary and also recovers the £10,000 shortfall, compared to the salary, from the first year. They keep growing their business for the next three years with £110,000, £130,000 and £150,000 turnover, so they conservatively make £40,000, £50,000 and £60,000 profit with the same margin but perhaps slightly higher operating costs. They then sell the business for £100,000. Five years later they have earned £75,000 more than they would have if they had stayed in the job and for a £25,000 investment sell for £100,000, less any costs due to the franchisor for a sale, so they make another £80-100,000 profit on the sale.

There is also the added security that an established franchise business has a value and a brand that customers can relate to, which maximises the chance of success. The value in the franchise fee is also an investment, so even franchisees who decide to sell their businesses after a few months should recover some, if not all, of the initial investment.

In my opinion, anyone considering starting a business should consider franchising as a viable option or, at the very least, see what is involved in starting a venture.

Franchisees should be 70% entrepreneurs. If they are 100% entrepreneurs, they won't be successful franchisees, because they will always be reinventing the wheel.

Alan Guinn

Where do I start? – The best places to look

Where indeed? Well, here is the good news: there are numerous places at your fingertips where you can research the options available to potential franchisees.

The internet provides almost too much information and if you are not careful it can give you too many options. This can cloud your view. Over the years I have met hundreds of potential franchisees and often the single reason why they refuse to make a decision is simply because they have contacted so many companies they cannot make up their minds which franchise to choose: they procrastinate and opt for the status quo as an employee with the security of a regular salary.

There are new internet sites created every year, each looking to attract franchise companies to buy advertising space, which is how they generate income. Competition is tougher now than last century, as roughly twice the number of franchise opportunities are available now than ten years ago.

These sites, or portals as they are called, promote franchise companies that advertise with them and when you complete an enquiry form the data captured is passed to the franchise company so the franchisor can email or speak to you directly, to entice you to a meeting.

Therefore out of courtesy to advertisers, and if you want to avoid unnecessary calls from franchisors, it is best to fill out the information request only if you have a real interest, otherwise you will be inundated with brochures, emails and calls at all times of the day and night. There are literally dozens of sites now and over the years I have tried most of them to generate interest in the franchise companies under my control, but I think the following ones are the best for you as a possible franchisee.

Which Franchise is excellent and contains an overview, case studies of real franchisees, investment levels and subdivides by category. All franchises on the site are bfa members, and so by definition have been accredited, which is added peace of mind for you. The address is www.whichfranchise.com

Franchise Direct is also good, with a variety of search options available. It isn't as comprehensive as others and has mainly detail on the concept overview and investment level; it is at www.franchisedirect.co.uk

Franchise Gator is a subsidiary of Microsoft and is a newer site to the UK. With all of the relevant information and an occasional testimony, it covers all the salient points. You can see this site at www.franchisegator.co.uk

Franchise Sales is also good, with hundreds if not thousands of franchise opportunities, again with various search options that takes you to a page of information and a 'request for more information' form. Try to look for a bfa member, for added peace of mind. This site is found at www.franchisesales.com

Many of the established names in franchise development have their own sites as part of their exhibitions, or monthly magazines, such as Franchise World, operated by Bob and Nick Riding for many years. The magazine has always been a window to the industry, with fewer paid glossy sections and frank and informative articles without the haze of images, and for me that ranks as number one for franchisees and franchisors alike. A selection of well known and established franchisors can be found on the associated site at www.franchiseworld.co.uk with other pages dedicated to news and information.

The Franchise Magazine is now over 25 years old and is part of the Franchise Development Services under the leadership of Roy Seaman. The magazine has stories, case studies and advertisements in abundance, with replicated and selected stories by franchisor sub-categories available on line at www.thefranchise magazine.net

Business Franchise Magazine is the official journal of the bfa with links to the four main franchise exhibitions in the UK that take place in London, Birmingham, Manchester and Glasgow, all of which are operated by Venture Marketing. The site www.businessfranchise.com is similar to the Franchise Magazine with stories, case studies and links to the Franchise Directory site with paid advertisers.

Making Money & What Franchise evolved during the 1990s in a similar style to the established publications. Partridge Publications has a wide range of magazines in its portfolio, which certainly helped Editor Jeff James get both of these franchise-specific front covers onto the news-stands in places like WH Smith and Tesco. I think the magazines introduced franchising to many people. Information on lots of different franchises can be found at www.makingmoney.co.uk and www.what franchisemagazine.co.uk

Even the tabloids have related sites. Both the Daily Express and Daily Mail print dedicated pages every week on available franchises as part of the news items.

Finally, the bfa has an online directory of members accredited to a standard, with case studies and biographies of each member so that you can browse from the comfort of your own home. It is useful to visit the sections on assistance at www.thebfa.org while researching for your "ideal franchise".

With franchise associations now established in lots of countries, the message for ethical franchising is now global. For more information about a franchise association in a particular country visit www.franchiseassociations.org and select the country for links to the local association web site.

There are many franchise sites available. One tip is to search through Google or Yahoo and select pages from the UK, to remove the overseas sites that pop up. A simple search on franchising is enough to find new-start and even resale opportunities.

The internet is now perceived as the ideal place to research franchising in any country. Try searching "Franchise Opportunities" in any search engine and limiting to "pages in the UK" or your location to get tothe best ranked sites!

So many to look at – Creating a shortlist that appeals to you

What floats your boat? If everyone answered with a comfortable response then many franchises would have never got off the ground in the last twenty years.

An innovative idea with a good market potential may be the most appealing factor when choosing a franchise. Twenty years ago who would have thought that a coffee shop selling a variety of lattes, mochas or an Americano with a soya option would survive at £2.00 a cup and charging £1.75 for a muffin! Today Starbucks, Costa and Nero rule the High Streets of this land and the shopping malls of the world.

Many new franchises have been launched during the last thirty years and plenty of the new franchisees who seized the opportunity to enter a new market became very wealthy.

Human nature is to stay in a comfort zone; to do and work at something you already know. That is why people seeking out a franchise often fall into the trap of looking for a job they have just left. They can't find a similar franchise, give up before they have started, and back they go to employment, often ruing the day they didn't "go it alone".

First, clear your mind and decide whether you would like to be out and about or to stay indoors at a fixed location. This decision will remove roughly half of the available options. Second, looking for something that appears interesting will further narrow the options available to you. It is important to understand what the concept is and, if it is attractive, keep it on the list for now; it may be the best option in the end.

It is now time to start researching, based on the answers to the questions you asked yourself and your family. Look at everything, discarding quickly the franchises that you really don't understand or those that you don't see yourself doing. For example you may wish to work alone, therefore discard a franchise that requires staff.

How much you are prepared to invest is crucial to your decision, especially with bank credit not as freely available as it was in the first seven or eight years of the millennium.

Consider whether a new franchise may be better as the market potential is greater in the early days compared to a system that develops into a multi-territory operation. This depends on the size of the whole market, the saturation of franchisees already trading, and competitors, of course. A franchise with 300 active operators may have crossover and limited potential compared to one with a mere 25. At the same time, see how many companies operate in the same market. This is an indicator of a good concept and one that has a market, albeit with a number of competitors already.

Once you have a number of potential business opportunities that interest you, request a prospectus either on line or by telephoning the franchisor direct. If you decide to telephone then the next section gives you an indication of what to expect from the franchisor.

Imagine lots of funnels, each with a question and less and less filtering through to the next funnel and the next question – open your mind to new ideas but be honest and rule out those franchises that don't fit your life and comfort zone!

First impressions – Contacting the franchisor

Most franchisors have a main contact for recruitment, which appears on advertisements and web sites. Ideally this is the person you should speak to but remember that that person may be interviewing or out with franchisees. If you only want an information pack sent this is ideal, and in exchange for your details a franchise company will happily send glossy information to you.

Not everyone has an electronic version of their prospectus and often franchisors have gone to a great deal of expense to provide a glossy brochure to woo you into their world, so don't expect that sending an email is all that you need do. Assume that the franchisor is interested in your enquiry and will want to speak with you in the future.

Being polite yourself is important; franchisors want good people and if you are evasive and arrogant they may decide from their first impression of you not to bother sending information!

Many potential franchisees quiz and question employees, but remember that employees probably have instructions from the franchise manager not to give information on, for example, what areas are available, how much people earn or what the investment is. This information is really best left for discussions with the franchise manager, so don't expect to get many answers.

When making a call be polite, treat others as you would like to be treated yourself – you will get more benefit from your efforts!

Remember that employees probably cannot answer every question, so ideally save questions for the franchise manager – this prevents frustration!

The glossy bit – Understanding the brochures

Many franchise companies will wince at this opening comment but, like it or not, it is true. Almost every franchise brochure is a copy or hybrid version of some other franchise company. The quality of the various brochures that you receive may be very different, and the words a little different, but they all contain the same information. It depends on the franchise company's budget and how professional it is. Some contain a plethora of inserted sheets and things to play with, such as interactive DVDs, while others are a version of Tolkien's Trilogy, many pages long. Alternatively, some are printed on a desktop and use word processor art and images with inkjet smudges!

A great glossy brochure does not always mean a fabulous franchise.

You should receive a brochure within three days, any longer is an indication of a slack operation. It is important to bear in mind that some franchisors will prefer not to send information and instead push to meet you first. Europeans, and especially the British people, don't like this very American approach and are often defensive, however remember that at this early stage you are under no obligation.

The selection of brochures you receive should include an overview of the company, its history, people involved, what the product or service is and no doubt an idea of costs, working capital and what you can expect to earn. The indication of profitability will always include a disclaimer in the small print; this is a legal requirement so don't be put off by this.

With a number of brochures in your possession, the best advice is to sit down at a time when *you can concentrate* on all of the literature without distractions. Create two distinct piles, these of real interest and those rejected. Once you have done this you will have a better idea of who you would like to talk to further and this also allows you to say "no" straight away to any follow-up call from a rejected franchisor. This leads to another observation which is a very British trait: saying "maybe" instead of "no thank you" leads to protracted correspondence and phone calls. Therefore, although it is an uncomfortable feeling, it is best to be honest straightaway if you really do not understand, or cannot see yourself operating in that business or market.

Some, if not all, brochures contain an application form of sorts, asking you to complete personal details and return the form to the franchisor. This form often contains a section concerning financial information, which is really there to see if you have adequate funds to start a business. It usually has a line for you to insert monthly outgoings and perhaps property details. This helps the franchisor to offer the best advice on bank borrowing. Try to be as honest as you can here, if not overly conservative with what you spend every month, as it can save a lot of heartache later if you avoid a car loan or a "buy now pay later" sofa or 3D television that has a first of many payments next year.

Make time to consider all of the brochures that you receive – read them thoroughly and make two piles, those of real interest and those rejected.

Be honest with the financial information requested, it can save you a lot of heartache later.

Second contact – Tell me more

After you return the form, expect a call within a few days to arrange a meeting to talk more with a representative. Where any suggested meeting takes place depends on how the franchisor operates the recruitment policy; it can be a meeting at the head office or a convenient location, say a local hotel.

Many franchisors will call you outside of normal office hours to avoid the potential conflict of interests if you are at work and therefore may not be able to talk openly, so don't be put off by a call at home in the evening. Many forms will have a "best time to call" question so that they know when to call you. If not, you might consider writing a suggested optimum time of day for a call back.

Franchisors often use a telephone interview, and it saves lengthy travel times to meetings. After a call you may decide that you don't feel the concept is really as attractive as you thought or the person you spoke to was not professional enough. If you appear non-committal then many franchisors will reject you as well at this time, rightly or wrongly.

Alternatively, if you have chosen a short list of interesting opportunities you can call the franchisor to arrange a meeting or perhaps ask a few more prudent questions as part of your research.

The best advice here is to ask questions, listen to the responses and absorb the information; nobody will expect you to decide at this time. Approach this type of research with an open mind as the franchisor will be aiming to achieve a meeting to sell the concept in more detail. Meetings at the head office are usually held during the working week for two reasons; first so that you can see the people at the head office and see who would be supporting you, and second to show your commitment that you are taking the concept seriously.

Conversations between potential franchisees and franchise recruitment staff often appear heated and abrasive. Human nature is primarily to defend, and in some cases attack from a defensive position. A potential franchisee may want answers and the franchisor, in protecting the business and current franchisees, may not fully answer the questions, at least until they have the chance to get a disclosure form signed, which is a common practice. Try to remember that trust is earned by both sides.

Over the years I have had many hundreds, if not thousands, of conversations with potential franchisees and thankfully only a few conversations have left me flabbergasted at the aggressive approach of the caller demanding information, refusing to meet until I have sold them right there on the phone. My usual response is to suggest that the franchise may not be for them if their "prove it to me attitude" is so clear. It all comes down to common courtesy, being treated the way you treat others.

Arranging a meeting close to you and not at the head office may be perfect, but remember that franchisors are busy building a network, so please try to keep the appointment and allow enough time, say two hours, to really get into the detail. Perhaps this meeting will be linked to a visit to a location already operating within the system. Ask how long the meeting will take and make sure you have enough time to accommodate a full meeting. I have had people arrive at a hotel for a meeting with fifteen minutes available as they have to get back to work; this is no good for either party.

With a meeting arranged you may receive a confirmation by email or letter and often a call the day before to make sure you are still coming. This is common practice so don't be offended if you feel the franchisor is getting "heavy", they are only managing their own time effectively.

Before you go to meet a franchisor it is wise to write questions down on a pad to take with you, questions such as the following ones that Nat West include on their bespoke franchise advice website

- *Is the franchise serving an established market, or has that market yet to be developed?*

- *Is the market expanding or declining?*
- *Is it seasonal?*
- *Does it depend on trading from highly-specialised sites?*
- *How strong is the competition?*
- *Is the franchise competitive in its market?*
- *What share of the market does it hold?*
- *Has the franchise been sufficiently tested and are its franchisees successful?*
- *Do the initial and ongoing fees represent good value for money?*
- *Do the on-going fees still leave the product or service competitive and provide enough profit to make the business worthwhile?*
- *Does the franchisor have sufficient financial and management resources to provide the support promised?*
- *Is the franchisor fair and ethical in all business dealings?*
- *Is the franchisor a member of the British Franchise Association and abide by their code of practice?*
- *In the event of the franchisor's failure are there alternative suppliers?*

For more information visit the Nat West website www.natwest.com/business/services/market-expertise/franchising

Be patient and remember that the information is often released gradually so that you can absorb the facts at each stage. Don't expect to see the inner workings of a franchise at the first meeting, but expect an overview of the benefits.

Eye to eye – The first meeting – ask and listen

Many potential franchisees and franchisors see the first meeting as the most crucial in any potential partnership. The meeting is normally an informal discussion, a two-way interview and a relationship building exercise not unlike two opponents sizing each other up in the ring before the fight.

As with all interviews the first few seconds will determine the outcome and decision on whether it is a potential fit going forward; the same happens in a social environment when you meet someone at a party, say.

Even though the meeting is an informal discussion it is a business meeting, so if the franchisor turns up in scruffy clothes and a ten year old ex-fleet car perhaps they are not as successful as they would like you to think. Likewise, if you turn up looking like you have had a night on the ale and have not had a chance to change your clothes, there's a good chance that the potential partnership horse has fallen out of the gate, not just at the first fence.

Assuming that the first impressions are favourable then the main part of the meeting will be a conversation with questions asked about you and your aspirations whilst your list of questions is addressed in turn.

The literature received may have provided written answers already; many franchisors provide this to allow you to consider the opportunity from the comfort of your own home. Asking again to obtain a more detailed answer is fully acceptable.

The first, and most common, question is how long the franchise has been operating, which leads to how many franchisees are operating and by definition how quickly the network has grown. Asking how many have left over the life of the franchise will provide you with a better understanding of the so-called churn of franchisees and, again by definition, the success rate under the system. I really cannot stress enough that you have to accept that franchising doesn't work for everyone. As Alan Guinn, franchise expert and CEO of the Guinn Consultancy, says "it's like geometry; some get it sooner, some get it later, some just don't get it."

Try not to dwell on failures but concentrate on achievers when making such a massive decision. Before you think that I am attempting to gloss over a negative point, allow me to explain a little further.

Finding out why people fail is important; when you ask the question you will receive an answer, usually combined with an excuse. The key to any franchisor's answer is their definition of what a failure is, which may appear to be a "cloak and dagger" answer.

There has to be a defined criterion, and so my definition of failure is someone who ceases trading, brings the van back, defaults on a lease and exits the network without any funds, thus loses his or her investment. Whatever the reason, they have failed in the venture. However, if I as franchisor manage to sell their area on, clear what is due to me from that individual and then generate even £1 to pass back, it is not a failure, even if the individual is left with a bank loan, overdraft or tax bill.

This may seem harsh as a benchmark rule, but if say I have done everything possible and still managed to sell their business, even at a lower value than they paid for it, I have done my bit. Don't forget that the initial fee covers the licence to trade and access to the know-how; once you have had training, office equipment, literature and other set-up costs the fee has gone and has no resale value because the franchisor will have to do the same for a replacement.

Here is a reality check certainly worth considering. If you invest say £20,000 and £7,000 is for training and support, then your business is worth £13,000, not £20,000. I see you shaking your head but remember that £7,000 is for training and support; it has no tangible value because a replacement has to pay for their own training, and you cannot sell it to them. The analogy I can use here is buying a house with the value paid and stamp duty on top. When you sell the house you cannot get the stamp duty back and the buyer will have to pay it again; even if you sell next day, you both pay.

Expect a variety of mitigating reasons, all of which are possible, with the onus generally placed on the individual franchisee who has departed, failure or not in the eyes of the franchisor. Reasons or excuses normally relate to the commitment of an individual, for example whether they managed to get out of bed in the morning, or if someone says they have adequate funds to pay the household bills while they set up the business in the first year or so; if this isn't true and they simply run out of money, then the franchisor has not failed them, they have failed themselves.

Whether the franchise is a bfa full, associate or provisional member is another indication of whether they conform to the code of conduct. Indeed the bfa web site www.thebfa.org provides a list of questions to ask of franchisors.

Find out who set up the franchise concept, whether they are still involved and who is on the support team. This will either give you confidence or put you off the concept.

Disclosing all – or at least some stuff!

In the UK, disclosing what some may class as negative information is currently not a legal requirement, however in parts of Europe and the US this disclosure is required under Federal Law.

The US document was originally known as in a UFOC (Uniform Franchise Offering Circular), and was changed to the FDD (Franchise Disclosure Document) in 2007 and became effective 1st July 2008. It is a lengthy document with almost everything you need to know about a franchise company, down to financial information and affiliated or parent companies

The FDD is fairly detailed and is not far off what UK franchisors use in their glossy literature; however it also states litigation cases, if any of the senior managers have been declared bankrupt, fees and much more information. A full list of what should be included in an FDD is available on www.en.

wikipedia.org/wiki/UFOC or by searching under Franchise Disclosure Document in any search engine.

Although this type of document is not required in the UK and most other European countries, some US owned franchises do disclose this information, probably to ensure all territories globally operate under the same internal system so if a problem arises they know they have complied, even if it is overseas.

Back to this side of the pond; in reality nothing beats asking questions of the person in front of you, as body language gives away so much. Look for the signs that tell you if someone is disguising the truth.

However, don't treat a meeting with contempt as there are some excellent franchise opportunities out there and remember that you are selling to them as well, so try not to be an arrogant closet lawyer looking to trip a genuine franchise manager up. This isn't "A Few Good Men" and you should be able to handle the truth – you just need to ask nicely, as Jack Nicholson would say.

Make a list of questions; use the bfa website to get an idea of the type of usual question to bolster your own list. Ask about people who have not succeeded and why but concentrate on the positives not the negatives of an opportunity.

You're going to charge me what? – Licence fees: what do I get for my money?

It is a sore subject for many franchisees, ongoing licence fees or royalties. If had a pound for every franchisee who at some stage has questioned the monthly cheque back to the franchisor I would be sunning myself in the Bahamas right now, reading a thriller instead of writing a guide exposing franchising.

Some have compared franchisees to children who become petulant teenagers and eventually rounded adults. Franchisors are the parents or perhaps role models. This analogy is a little vague, so maybe a little more explanation is needed to get the point across; new franchisees need the help, guidance and mentoring from the franchisor, or in this case the parents. As the franchisee develops they find new ways to do things, question the franchisor much the same as a teenager rebels against Mum and Dad. At some stage though, most franchisees who stay in a network develop a level of appreciation for what the franchisor has done, again much like the way that twenty-somethings start saying thanks to parents who have supported them through university, work and life in general. Then at "twenty something", as a young adult versus an ageing parent, they may not always agree but the discussion is usually less confrontational, more level headed and becomes a debate rather than an argument.

Before you enter into agreements, or even read past this chapter, you need to understand and accept that licence fees have a place in franchising.

Licence fees vary from company to company; some are based on turnover with a percentage set and contracted when you enter the franchise agreement. Normally this is a standard rate for every franchisee but in some cases new-start franchise companies may have offered a lower rate to help establish the network and you may see an increased rate compared to longer serving franchisees. Don't be put off by this: it is fairly common and isn't the franchisor ripping you off.

Cap in hand

Most franchisors have adopted capping levels so that when you get to a pre-agreed turnover the maximum or capped licence fee is the royalty due. Capping licence fees is a way of rewarding you for achievement and allows you to take 100% of the turnover for growing the business over and above the capped level.

It is not unusual that capped schemes are offered after a qualifying period, say a year in business. Occasionally the option to join a capped or fixed fee is offered by the franchisor immediately, which may appear attractive to you if this is the case. However, agreeing to a capped fee usually means that you pay the whole amount from the first month of trading, irrespective of turnover achieved.

Capped schemes are strict because both franchisors and franchisees have attempted scams in the past, such as topping and tailing sales figures. Some franchisees submitted a high figure one month, which was capped, and then a low figure the next and paid the set licence fee percentage, then high then low and so on. Franchisors are not stupid, and this is why modern schemes usually mean that when you join a capped scheme you pay the fixed cap fee from the first month. The modern schemes do allow franchisees to withdraw from the scheme but then stipulate that you cannot rejoin for a year or so. The strict schemes available today avoid the game-playing element of trying to dodge licence fees.

Jim'll fix it

Other franchise operators charge a fixed licence fee no matter what turnover you achieve. This is normally a token amount but is charged even if you turn over a pound.

Gratis – almost

There are a number of opportunities available that don't charge any ongoing licence fees, Utopia for both parties with no real need to audit your business and make sure you are paying your dues. I have offered advice to a number of newer franchise businesses and the attraction for potential franchisees is huge when you line up against 5%, 7.5% and even 20% royalty companies. In reality this means either a higher upfront franchise fee or higher costs prices for products bought under exclusive licence from the franchisor.

The best advice here is to understand that a serious franchisor is not going to be satisfied in selling you an area, taking your money and leaving you to it. They need to benefit from your success, extend the use of products or services via a network and in turn take a cut of your sales through a percentage of sales, capped fees, fixed fees or additional margin in the products they provide.

If committing to ongoing royalty payments is uncomfortable for you then perhaps franchising isn't the right option as you consider self employment. I always remind potential franchisees that for the ongoing fees they will receive support, access to innovative ideas, association with a brand and enjoy the benefits of being in a network. These all cost money to provide and the additional income from the fees goes towards covering that cost.

Weigh up the type of licence fees charged and make sure that you understand the ongoing fees for the term of the agreement. Ask if capping schemes are available and how you qualify to join such scheme in the future.

Take a good hard look in the mirror – Is franchising for me, or indeed us?

At this stage, perhaps after months of research and a first meeting with a possible partner, you will probably have a pile of paperwork, a copy of the franchise agreement and a list of answers to questions that you have asked.

The next question that you must ask yourself is whether franchising is really right for you and your family. The answer to this question is found inside of each individual and will not be found in any book or website.

Franchising is a concept, a way of life and a commitment like no other in the employment market. It provides individuals with the independence of running their own business allied to the security of having support from an experienced mentor and the comfort factor that other franchisees are in the same position.

I guarantee that you will have the following if the franchisor has done their job properly;

- Established franchisor
- Good training
- Great concept
- Abundant market possibilities
- Freedom
- Value for my investment
- They are nice people ...

If your list has all of the above and a few more hopefully, then give yourself a pat on the back. However, if it has only two or three benefits then there may be something missing.

After meeting thousands of people considering franchising I find it difficult not to prejudge and often a wry smile appears on my face at the same time as a recurring thought that is similar to one that any salesperson has every day; the simple judgement that the person in front of me would prefer not to make a decision at all!

I don't mean to sound flippant or judgemental here, as I have been that person on many occasions, standing there attempting to decide on which leather sofa to buy, the chocolate or cream one, to spend this much or that much, shall I try another furniture shop? No decision is the right decision, for today at least!

What do you think darling?

Making a decision is a very singular event. Although we may consider the opinion of others, eventually the final call is down to the individual. Of course if the franchise is a business where you and your partner will work together it will be a joint decision. Even if this is not the case a life partner has very important input to any decision. Ideally the whole family needs to be almost 100% convinced or problems will occur later at home.

The best advice for any couple considering working together is to set the parameters early: by that I mean talk and discuss the worst case scenario, financially and personally, and agree that the risk is acceptable. If the risk is not acceptable, perhaps working together is not a viable option.

A compromise may be to have one start the business while the other stays in gainful employment until the business can sustain both. This has inherent problems if the employed partner, the bread winner, feels pressure at having to go to work while the other has the fun in the new venture. So, discuss this as well.

If you haven't read "Men are from Mars, Women are from Venus" it may be worth doing so to give you an insight into the mindset of the other sex. Notwithstanding the assumption of the stereotypical male and female couple, the same is true for same sex partners and even friends and relatives working and living together.

The fact remains that more men go into franchising, although this imbalance is changing as more women consider franchising now. Society still sees the man as the bread winner; however this is another impression that is changing. No matter who is perceived to be the bread winner in the family unit, the person who adopts this role should take heed of the advice from Jim Rohn, one of the world's most respected business advisors and mentor. Sadly Jim passed away in 2009 but his work, advice and legacy remain; his messages continue to be promoted today by Jim Rohn International.

Rohn stresses the importance of looking after "you" first as the priority of life. This may sound selfish to some, but he then asks a question: if you cannot look after "you" then how "can you look after anyone else?" In fact Rohn used a humorous example in his talks, painting a picture for his audience of a common airline flight when the captain releases the oxygen masks, asking the audience what they should do next. "Do you put a mask on your child or the person next to you?" After a pregnant pause the audience catches up and perhaps picture the stewardess' pre-flight advice that we probably know off by heart today, and he says "no–no, put your mask on first, then help others." How true.

So Rohn isn't being selfish or chauvinistic, he is absolutely right in the advice to look after you, as a first priority. After that you will be stronger and more competent in looking after your partner, children and others.

If you haven't read or heard any of Jim Rohn's work it is certainly worth a look at www.jimrohn.com

I digress, but with reason: understanding the psychology behind making a life-changing decision is a whole different subject and would take up a few chapters at least.

Get a piece of paper and rule a line down the middle – write the positive points on one side and the negative points on the other side, then decide whether the negative points can be turned into positive points with help from the franchisor. If they can great, if not you have to decide whether the positive points are strong enough to help you make a decision at all.

Let's get formal – The second meeting – let's talk detail

At this stage nobody expects that you have made a final decision, far from it. However if you decide to move forward to a second meeting with a particular franchise company there's a very good chance that you have eliminated some opportunities. From the relatively informal discussion of the first meeting you should expect a more formal second meeting, with more information offered. The franchisor will often aim to get some form of provisional commitment, so expect some direct questions and you may even be asked for a deposit to secure your area. This is common practice and you should really expect some "sales closing techniques" before you go to the meeting.

Detail is the key for this meeting; it normally revolves around three key areas, territory, agreement and ideal start dates. From this discussion both parties will have an understanding of where, how and when.

Territory is usually the first subject and takes a look at the map of your preferred area. If the franchisor has done a good job he will be prepared and have demographics ready to highlight the market and potential in the defined territory. This assumes that the franchisor has a territory programme, as some actually don't work on exclusive areas. If they don't then make sure that you ask how many more franchisees they have or intend to have in your area.

Question the demographics, if presented, and make sure they are relevant to your business. There is no point in having a vast area, say Cumbria, with a population of so many thousand and 80% in Carlisle, for example, if you are opening a print shop. Better to have a confined area in Carlisle and 100% of that population, or even half of it so that you can concentrate on the south side and hope another franchisee joins and together you can develop the brand north and south of the city.

Resales

At this stage the franchisor may introduce a resale area close to you. Don't be alarmed, as this could be a golden opportunity with a customer base in place and in turn probably income from day one. Often a franchisor will offer a low turnover area for the same price as a virgin area, to move a low-performing franchisee out quickly. As long as this isn't a regular occurrence on the area in question it may be a good opportunity for you, so delve into the history, find out how many franchisees have been on that area and why it is for sale.

Often new franchise concepts offer large areas to franchisees in an attempt to lure them into a perceived huge slice of the country. Land grab, as it is referred to, is not a real advantage because usually these huge areas are underdeveloped, with a really small market penetration with vast mileage covered every year to secure customers far, far away.

Poaching

Territory disputes are rare but do occur when a neighbouring franchisee poaches on another one's patch. It may be wise to ask the franchisor if there is any business currently covered by another franchisee on the territory you are considering and what will happen when you start. Most of the time this is passed over to you as a bonus; however regulation of trade means that it is not always enforceable by the franchisor.

Harmony normally reigns and neighbouring franchisees see the benefit of helping each other and so the poaching is normally resolved amicably.

The Contract

The second meeting dedicates a lot of time to the contract. It may be that you have already had a copy from the first meeting and already have a franchise savvy solicitor pulling it apart; indeed if this is the case the second meeting may revolve around clarification of a number of points.

However, if you are presented with a copy at the second meeting, expect to see a bulky document that has a lot of clauses and jargon. Don't expect to understand the detail at the meeting but expect a brief overview from the franchisor. The salient points will be what you need to do and what the franchisor will do for you. A good franchise agreement will be fair to both sides, although expect a number of clauses heavily in favour of the franchisor so that they can protect the network and the integrity of the brand, or intellectual property as it is referred to. There will be a breakdown of the costs charged and it should itemise the set-up equipment, if any is provided, as well as training commitments made by the franchisor.

A good franchisor will explain in layman's terms the inclusion of various clauses and should not be embarrassed by any point.

If there is a concern with a clause or constraint, then discuss it with the franchise manager and request clarification if it appears ambiguous. A written confirmation is a great document to have later if there is a difference of opinion on a clause during the life of your agreement.

Many years ago franchisees did not even take legal advice, however even though today most agreements are standard and not negotiable, it is best policy for a franchisor to suggest that a franchisee takes advice; there are even clauses included that make sure the franchisee has acknowledged this advice, born out of legal cases. Whether you take advice or not is entirely up to you. If you do, judge any cautionary points raised by a solicitor carefully. Remember that solicitors have to raise the points to save possible negligence claims in the future. In reality, if every client stood by every recommendation the world would not have agreements or contracts at all, because stalemate would occur at every negotiation.

Start Dates

Discussing start dates is a normal part of the second meeting. Training course dates are normally mentioned by a franchisor to gain a form of commitment from you, a buying signal for the franchisor. Be honest here: if you are going to start but for some reason cannot do so for six months, let the franchisor know. Making a commitment does not mean entering into the agreement though, it merely means that you might reserve a territory and put a deposit down, which is absolutely normal.

There are two types of deposit: refundable and non-refundable. In my opinion the refundable deposit is only a psychological commitment; it means nothing and in truth is a soft sell used by franchisors. Asking for the money back, if you change your mind, normally results in a "high level" sales pitch to try to turn you around and recommit.

The benefit for you as a franchisee is that you can secure the territory and your place with a low-risk option while looking at finance options, for example.

Many companies use the non-refundable technique, which is a real commitment. By definition, you will secure a territory and have a period of time to arrange finance, give notice at work and maybe even fit a family holiday in before the big start date. Most deposit schemes allow 90 days from the date of the deposit and three months to start your training. However, read the small print; if you go over this and there isn't a provision for extending the period, you may forfeit the fee. The reason for the clause is that some people actually pay and disappear. The time limit then allows the franchisor to place the territory on the market again.

Don't be afraid to ask very direct questions, this is a very important decision!

Now go away and think about it – Be 90% sure

With the second meeting finished, you may have committed in some way with a deposit, but even if this is the case you have not signed a contract and the worst case scenario is that you will lose your deposit.

After the meeting, potential franchisees often have a feeling of euphoria, being completely fired up and impatient to get started. The dream for many, to be their own boss, is well within their grasp. Even though you might have this emotion you really have to be sure, so the next few days are very important.

No matter how sure you are, doubt will creep in as you start to question yourself; it is human nature. It may be a friend in the pub who comments on the market, or even your skills to run a business. Great friend! You might find yourself regurgitating the benefits explained to you in the second meeting, arguing the case and selling the concept to your friend. That is a good sign; however, if you start to agree then perhaps there is a problem, especially if you can argue any of the points raised. My advice here is to pick the phone up and ask your contact at the franchise, don't let it fester.

Not much more really needs to be said in this section. It is very personal and you really need to be 90% sure that it is right. How you measure this is down to you but it is fine to have a few doubts so don't expect to be 100% sure, it rarely happens.

Try to make a decision quickly, a few days at most. The longer you take to make a decision the more chance that doubt will creep in and prevent you making a decision at all.

3

Getting Serious

Sorting out the Legalities

Time for independent advice

And this is what I will do –
Creating a solid business plan

Potentially you have been sold on a really good concept, you have visualised yourself in business, successful, cash rich and maybe even arriving at work in a nice Aston Martin Vanquish instead of the family car. It's a nice warm feeling every time you think about being the next Mister or Miss Big.

Time for a reality check. To get to the vision takes a bit of planning and lots of hard work. Please don't think it is a straight swap for a cheque.

Creating a business plan is essential, working the numbers for you as an individual; remember that you are unique.

If you have had the luxury of developing business plans in a previous life then the skills will certainly help, but if not don't panic. People will help you if you need a little bit of assistance.

First stop is the bank, which may have a template for you to fill in so that you and they understand the figures. If not, the second stop is the franchisor who also may have a template.
Putting your own plan together is a great business tool; it really focuses the mind and gives you something with which to measure your developing business later.

A third option available in the UK is to use an independent company, such as Franchise Finance. They are members of the bfa and work with a number of franchisors as well as individuals to help create business plans and assist in obtaining finance. For more information visit www.franchisefinance.ltd.uk

"How to" guides are available at the library, online and from Business Link, but in truth a business plan is quite a simple thing to create, using a word processing programme and spreadsheet programme. Microsoft Word and Excel are the best known ones, however other spreadsheet software is available with similar programmes that work perfectly well. If you don't use Microsoft software it is a good idea to check that your software is compatible with Excel as most people use Microsoft software.

Getting started is the hardest part but once the programme is open, following simple rules can save you time and effort. The key ones are below.

- Use formulas to allow you to change parts quickly
- Don't forget (if they apply)
    - Vehicle leases and tax (any deposits)
    - Fuel and insurance
    - Accountant's costs
    - All telephones – including mobiles
    - Rent increases and deposits
    - Extras – include a line for miscellaneous costs
    - Product wholesale costs
    - Post and carriage charges
    - Advertising and Website
    - Staff Wages – don't forget National Insurance contributions
    - Bank loan repayments and charges
    - Stationery
    - Licence fees payable

Many franchisors will help you with this. They will have profit examples available showing what you can achieve, and they may even email you a blank version so that you can insert your own figures.

What you will probably see is a real idea of what will be available every month, but don't forget that profit is not the same as cash. Customers may want credit, hopefully not but it is a consideration, while your suppliers may also offer you some credit. Again, a franchisor worth their salt will have a cash example as well, including VAT and credit terms with the impact on what is in your bank account at the end of a month.

With this complete information, based on assumption of course, you have a plan and the cash availability and this will show you what overdraft you may need or what cash you will need to inject into the business to keep it solvent.

A word of advice here: add at least £5,000 to the requirement, to take the pressure off. Over the years I have sat down with many franchisees who were in the doldrums after running out of money, having worked to a plan based on assumptions to the penny with nothing held in reserve. Perhaps a customer had not paid to terms or an emergency at home had taken them out of the business for a week and scuppered the sales figures. Do yourself and your family a favour and build in a contingency reserve for unexpected situations.

When you have finished the plan, read it a few times just to make sure that you really have a good idea of all the costs and how you intend to get business. It is a good idea to run it past a friend, perhaps a business owner, so that they can give you some advice or hopefully praise you on a well thought out plan.

Do the maths! Assume a slow start and higher costs, but remember that a plan has to have a contingency – try to keep £5,000, or enough to pay your personal bills, aside for at least 3–6 months to take the pressure off.

Sell your story – Talking to the banks and getting adequate finance

Starting a business needs some involvement from a bank. Even if you don't need a loan or overdraft you will need a business account, at the very least.

The good news is that most of the High Street banks in the UK have a dedicated franchise team or department to help franchised business owners. It makes commercial sense for the banks to lend to people who will follow a system whilst developing their business.

Nat West and RBS are effectively the same organisation now and the team really knows all there is to know about franchise operators in the UK. They are active and visit franchisors regularly to find out what progress is being made, obtain feedback about how many franchisees have been recruited in the last year, and more than likely even look at the most recent audited accounts. What Nat West does with this information is the important bit. The information is fed into the intranet system so when you see your local branch manger he can have a look at the internal rating that the team has given a particular franchise opportunity. Established franchisors with a proven and sustained record of success will rate well while new unproven systems may not even have a rating.

The good bit for you as a franchisee is that it may speed up a decision from the bank and save you from waiting. Lending is entirely dependent on the rating and credit risk systems employed at a particular time and suitable security, such as your house or other assets, may be required.

On average, the banks provide around 70% of the cost to set up your business, so if the total set-up cost is say £30,000 then the bank will fund £21,000, leaving you to find £9,000.

It is usual for banks to consider a mixture of overdraft and business loan to spread the repayment over a number of years.

HSBC and Lloyds TSB are also very active in the industry and provide a similar system to Nat West. Indeed HSBC sponsors a number of industry events, such as the Franchisor of the Year.

Banking has changed considerably over the last three decades, with an emphasis on selling services, insurance policies and pensions. Banks want your business so that they can offer you a plethora of added extras.

If you believe in your plan and have adequate security, getting finance is a little easier than approaching a bank with a non-franchise business idea, especially if the franchisor is established.

It is important to mention that this is not the same for every country and each one has their own lending criteria for franchising. Banks are increasingly cautious after the near collapse of some banks worldwide that required government intervention. Some did not survive the crash and unfortunately some of those that did go were the main franchise financiers, for example CIT in the US. This has since had a detrimental effect on those seeking finance in the US, which may take years to improve.

Remember that banks want your business and they want to help, but also remember that the High Street business teams might not have the expertise so contact the franchise team direct if you are really serious about moving forward.

Family life – Understanding the impact on personal finances

The next big consideration is the money you need to pay the household bills. These are not business related, of course, but consideration of the financial impact at home of a new venture is definitely a part of the process when you are creating a solid business plan. It is no different from balancing the books when you have a salary coming in, but remember that with a business your salary payment will not be assured.

I really cannot stress how important this consideration is, but don't think that I am being negative or anal; it is just as important for a franchisor to ensure that you are aware of these considerations and that you can cover the bills so that you can develop your business without additional distractions.

Starting a business has an effect on the family; longer hours may mean that children don't see their mother or father as much. Saturday may be a working day, especially if the new business is retail or food orientated.

Whatever the impact or potential impact, it is always a good idea to sit down as a family and talk about what you have decided to do and why.

One thing to remember is next year. Setting up a business often means that taking two weeks out for a family holiday is not viable, especially when you are a sole trader. If your new venture involves employing staff, then taking a break may be easier, however that means getting reliable staff and making a decision to leave them in charge.

Two weeks on the beach is, for most, a sacrifice for the first couple of years. How you get round this may be a few shorter breaks or a week over traditionally quieter periods, such as just before Christmas or around other seasonal times. This is completely down to what franchise you are looking at. If it is retail, no time is a quiet time, hopefully.

Nugget... in a Nutshell

Try to build in definite family time and even time for you to recharge your business batteries.

At this stage, before you sign up, make sure that family and friends know what you are signing up to – manage their expectations as well.

Each franchise is different; some have staff while others are a man and a van. What is important is to know that with good planning and an understanding and supportive family, quality time and harmony are completely possible.

What am I signing up to? – Get the franchise agreement checked

In the previous chapter I mentioned the need to get the fundamental clauses explained to you. However, I also made it quite clear that most franchise agreements are uniform and it serves no purpose for franchisors to add to or amend the standard agreement, save the specific area details and your details. In reality, if you have already seen a franchise savvy solicitor and have discussed any points raised then you will be ready to sign up, but be aware that solicitors often advise you not to sign anything. This is the nature of the beast, the professional make-up of a lawyer, and without being critical it is what lawyers do every day. They make arguments, receive responses and counter-argue until, after an exchange of views, a compromise is reached. This process falls down when a uniform agreement is not negotiable and in order to protect the ethical best advice, a lawyer may advise you not to sign up, just in case you fall foul to that clause in the future and sue them for bad advice.

Having an agreement looked over is not cheap and can cost anything from £300 to £1000, but a cautionary piece of advice is definitely needed here. I strongly suggest that you don't take a franchise agreement to a High Street solicitor who carries out conveyance for the most part. Franchise lawyers, such as Field Fisher Waterhouse and Hamilton Pratt, write and act on behalf of franchisors and franchisees every day and are the best to consider.

It is important to remember that this is a blanket agreement and it covers the whole network. It probably cost the franchisor many thousands of pounds to have it written and updated and the legal advice is that it is fair and up to date. A change may not be possible as it may render another franchisee's contract void. Any established franchisor will attempt to explain why a clause is written a certain way and will stand their ground thereafter. It's a bit like Henry Ford when asked what colour people could have their new automobiles in; his reply was "you can have any colour you like as long as it's black."

Be cautious of a franchisor that is happy to remove clauses or reword something just to get you to sign up. To put this into perspective, try to imagine being part of the network and two years later a new franchisee does something that isn't in the best interests of your business in the next territory. You may complain to the franchisor and expect them to use the clause that is in your own contract to resolve the clear breach of a clause only to find that it is not enforceable as the rogue franchisee demanded it be removed. Franchise agreements protect the network as well, and must be uniform.

Of course take advice and consider any points flagged by your lawyer; that is what you should do. However, if the points relate to a chain of events, such as if you don't pay a bill, make a return and continue to breach conditions, well guess what? You may lose your investment! In reality though, paying a bill a day late will not mean termination of your agreement because a franchisor would never enforce such a ridiculous condition. What they do need is a clause that allows them to act if a franchisee is a regular late payer or non-payer.

Try to remember that taking a franchise is a partnership and although parameters are needed at the start, in most cases the franchisor will work with you to develop your business which, in turn, will develop the brand name and reputation of their business. Ask yourself why any franchisor would want to sign anyone up and then spend months or years arguing just to enforce a clause, terminate your agreement and then sell the area again just to start the arguments again.

Final decision time – Be 90% sure

If after this you are 90% sure, great, 95% sure, fantastic, but as I have said already, don't expect to be 100% sure as it rarely happens.

If you have real problems with any clauses in the contract speak to other franchisees and see how it has impacted on their business. Think not how a clause could hurt me but rather how a clause could protect me!

Once you have decided, then commit and let the contact at your chosen destiny know. You are ready to start the rest of your life. Finance is in place, the family is aware and supports your decision, and you are ready to sign the agreement and arrange your training. How exciting.

4

No Turning Back

Committing to your Decision

Putting pen to paper

You sign here – Contracts time

Most franchisors prefer to meet you in person to sign an agreement, although it is not unheard of for an agreement to be sent via courier or by post for you to sign. I find this a little mechanical, however it works for some companies. Personally I think that if someone has committed to joining an organisation then at the very least someone from the executive team should get into a car, onto a plane or train, and welcome a new partner into the fold.

Meeting in person allows further discussion on a variety of subjects, all covered in this chapter, as well as the psychological effect of someone shaking your hand and enthusing about your new venture.

Signing a contract doesn't need a notary witness and the contract is normally signed by one of the executive team on behalf of the franchisor while you sign as either a director or sole trader. A few years ago there was a problem in the industry with some rogue elements that signed contracts as limited companies, which was fine at the time. However when disputes occurred they terminated the agreement and used the knowledge to set up as independent traders under their own name. A limited company is a separate legal entity and, once dissolved, the contracts affected were in fact only with a paper entity. The result was that the franchisors could not enforce clauses prohibiting trade in any area and there were a few red faces.

To combat this problem franchisors flocked to all parts of their networks in the UK and overseas and sought to add personal covenants for those trading as limited companies. Most were successful, however some franchisees saw this as an escape route and, well the rest is history best confined to the archives of individual companies.

Soon after these events, new contracts included personal covenants whilst accepting the franchisees' right to set up limited companies for tax benefits as well as personal limitation on risk.

Today, expect a personal compliance clause which may even offer extensions to any director or employee. Now you know why it is included.

Franchise contracts, or agreements, are updated regularly as a matter of course and especially when new legislation is passed. The only difference that your agreement has compared to that of any other franchisee in the network is the schedule, which is specific for a defined area if the franchisor includes territories. The franchisor will explain all of the items at the time and will confirm what you receive as your set-up package.

When you sign the agreement you might be asked to initial each page as well as the specific schedules relating to your area and your training or set-up package. Initialling each page is totally normal and an action that has evolved only over the last few years, probably because of a litigation case that relied on evidence of no initial. Who knows?

Once you have decided to sign up do it sooner rather than later and start as soon as you can.

If for any reason you have an undertaking from the franchisor outside the standard agreement, get this added to the schedule section at the end.

How much do I owe? – Paying the balance

The final bit will be to hand over the cheque for the balance. Instead of a cheque it may be a bank draft or confirmation of the funds transfer made using internet banking or a branch-generated electronic transfer.

There may be agreement for you to pay the balance at a later date, which may be just before the training course. However, don't forget that, even if this is the case, once you have signed the agreement you are bound by the terms and commitment to pay the full balance.

With funds transferred or to follow, and contracts signed, you are a franchisee. Congratulations!

When is the next course? – Arranging start date

With the contract signed you will be chomping at the bit to get started, and so you should.

It is more than likely that start dates and training courses will have been discussed long before you signed the contract, but if not then confirming dates at the signing ceremony may even depend on other factors such as release of funds by the bank or building society, or even notice periods for employers. Franchisors are fairly flexible; of course they want you to start as soon as possible but if you have to defer to a later course this is never a problem as long as the fees are paid by the original time agreed when signing the contract.

Informing an employer can be a difficult experience for some. Resisting the temptation to tell someone to insert the job in an orifice is difficult, and many have failed, but if it could affect final salary payments and the cash needed for the plan, try to hold your tongue – at least until the last official day! Although many employers are sad to see good staff go, I am glad to say that in my experience most employers are extremely supportive and helpful. There are some who bleed every last minute of the notice period. I have never understood this policy and person-ally I have not imposed anything remotely similar in any of the businesses that I have run over the years. Making someone work when their attention and motivation are obviously elsewhere is damaging, in my opinion. Although collating valuable knowledge is important for the continuity of any business, there is a limit. It is far better to set out a brief period to hand over information, maybe introduce key clients to a new account manager or suppliers to a new purchase contact, but thereafter I have let people go with a simple request: "if we need some help or can't find some information, can we call you?" The answer has always been yes and makes sense; keeping communication open is critical and far outweighs churlish actions.

If you are leaving a job resist the temptation to walk away and risk final salary due, even if your employer is being churlish. Smile and bite your lip and get what you are entitled to, because every penny counts when you start to work for yourself.

Better start preparing – Things you can do before training

Preparation is a very important part of any business venture and the time between signing your contract and the training date is as valuable as any time after training starts.

There may be a need to spend time with landlords, builders and even solicitors to ensure a premises-based franchise is ready for the franchisor's bit if they are providing shop fitting as part of the bundle of set-up costs included in the fee. This will be your first real experience of the support function and a good franchisor will handle the whole project, at arm's length perhaps, with advice on what to do and when.

Franchisors sometimes engage in a pre-launch programme working with you before the training course on marketing plans so that you hit the ground running, straight after training and the official launch in your area. Expect some interaction from new names that are part of the support team, from the Franchise Director to Managing Director's secretary, who might call you about progress with bank accounts, any forms that may require completing or even a call to just to make sure you have received accommodation details.

There may be a need to order stationery in advance of your course and so the support team may be in contact for VAT registration numbers. This links nicely to the things that you need to do when becoming self-employed. The process of applying for a VAT number and registering with the Inland Revenue (HMRC) or relevant governing bodies is well documented in a number of websites such as www.direct.gov.uk Legislation is ever changing so a definitive check list in this book may become outdated and inaccurate very quickly – assuming I sell enough copies to warrant a second impression that is! Seriously, thresholds and limits change almost every year and so the franchisor should tell you what you need to do.

If the new venture involves the supply of products then you may ask for or be given some information to digest before the training course. If the products are for commercial or industrial use then you may see product data sheets that explain use, precautions and health and safety data. If this is the case, don't worry if you see warning symbols; panic need not set in if you see a skull and crossbones! If a health and safety sheet was written for water it would have warnings like "do not inhale."

If you do get this type of information then it really makes sense to take some time to read it a few times, and not the night before the course starts. If you do I promise you the first day will be far less daunting.

How much or how little involvement there is in between signing up and starting is different for each franchise. There is no right or wrong as long as you are ready to start at 9.00 a.m. on the first day of training. Constant interruptions to give someone a VAT number, telephone numbers, or call from solicitors regarding the lease don't help you or your fellow trainees. If these distractions can be avoided then you will have a free mind to learn your new trade.

It is a great idea to get in your car and drive to different parts of your territory, whether a defined area or not, to get an idea of who your future customers might be.

Spending a little time sourcing types of companies that are core business for your new venture is another way of preparing to launch your franchise.

It is strange but true that you start to see new things and opportunities once you begin franchising. A farm shop with a tea room might be a nice client if you suddenly see it as a user of your products. The industrial estates that you once drove past now draw you in to see who does what and how you can help reduce their costs if, say, your new business is a cost analysis franchise. The list of examples could go on and on.

Ask for product information from your new business partner and start to learn what your new business is all about.

Get to know the territory and take a few different turns from your usual route to find little gems hidden away!

5

Back to the Classroom
Initial Training OMG!

Now write this down and remember it!

Be a sponge – The induction training starts

Most training courses start on Monday, so if you are close to the venue then an early start to beat the traffic is needed, best not to be late for your first day!

Even if you are close to the training venue it really is worth considering staying over with other franchisees, not only to experience the social integration of a complete course but to let you concentrate completely on the course.

For those too far away to commute it is likely that the franchisor has made arrangements for you to lodge in a hotel for the duration of the course.

Some international franchisors carry out training overseas. For example Signarama flies people from all over the world to West Palm Beach in Florida for the training course. The Signarama courses are two weeks long and that means flying on Saturday to arrive late that day with a day to recover before training on Monday. The middle weekend involves a Saturday morning session, and then a bit of recreational time in the Sunshine State before the second week starts. On Friday afternoon people leave for all corners of the world before launching their store the following week, in most cases.

It isn't a holiday by any means and most of the time is spent in the classroom learning all aspects of the business as well as meeting various support people from the Home Office Stateside team. It is one of the most intensive and "feel good" courses out there and by the end of the two weeks you can feel invincible, with new friends from all over the world.

For most European franchises, a course begins in a decent hotel on that Sunday. If you are attending a residential course then it is a good idea to get a list of fellow rookies, so that you can keep in touch, meet for a drink in the bar and maybe even have dinner on Sunday evening.

Whatever the travel arrangements, the first day of training is similar to starting a new job so if you are a little apprehensive this is understandable. Try to relax and remember that everyone wants you to succeed. Don't be surprised if you see the franchise manager in the dining room; it is common for people to turn up and join you, sometimes unannounced.

Any well planned course has a proven agenda and this is normally explained by the trainer in the first few minutes. A good course will be balanced between practical and theory sessions, with regular breaks.

If your new venture is product based you will have plenty of sessions explaining the characteristics and benefits of each product, or at least a selection of the main products. If it is a manufacturing styled venture then expect a number of practical sessions that show you how to make the end product. If it is purely a service, for example an accountancy or business cost-saving service, then expect sessions on what to do to adapt any business into the bespoke system or find savings in various cost centres.

Any good agenda will also have sessions on sales, finance, administration and insurance. Some of these may seem boring, especially if you crave the hands-on practical playtime, but remember that they all interlock into the system that you have bought into. Be a sponge and welcome every session as a crucial part of your knowledge quest.

Getting the most out of a training course depends on your involvement and that of fellow rookies, which leads me to some things to look out for from trainers and other new starters. Try to remember that although everyone cannot be a great presenter or orator, the trainer may be an excellent one-to-one communicator or telephone support person. Don't judge someone's ability to relay a relatively boring subject to you in an enthusiastic manner. Keeping financial records isn't the most earth-moving experience for most of us, no matter how much you spice it up.

Spotting the wildlife – Training room mammals

Do you remember your schooldays and the pupil that disrupted the class with witty comments, well witty to them, and the effect on the lesson? Well sometimes these people grow up to be older versions of the class fool.

For some reason they are attracted to franchising, and although most get spotted at the interview stage there are times when they get through the selection process and end up on training courses. You may be unfortunate and find a version on your course, so I warn you they come in a few different mammalian species.

The Know All

The first is the "Know All" who has sold snow to Eskimos, been the best salesperson for every job they have had. Questioning every sales technique presented, they may mock those in the class who have not sold before and attempt to scare them as well.

Any good sales trainer will spot this species and nip the negativity in the bud. An astute franchisor will use the model to help others in a constructive way and if this fails they may knock them down a peg or two, openly or covertly. If you do get this type ignore them, because most of the time they are set in their ways and will find it difficult to adapt to the franchise.

The Kamikaze

Species number two is the "kamikaze", although not a divine wind, far from it. They often ooze negativity and question everything as less than perfect, with a blinkered animosity for the franchise they have just signed up to.

Although they are the most disruptive type in a classroom environment they can really motivate fellow classmates who get annoyed with the negative effect on the group. In most cases the franchisor will address this head on. In my experience a quiet chat sets the tone for the rest of the partnership and, if handled properly, the self destruct kamikaze tendencies can be reversed before the model nose dives into the company ship.

The Rabbit

Species number three is the "rabbit" that freezes in front of the self-employed headlights. Easy to recognise, they looked scared to death in every session and freeze in sales role play activities. Less disruptive than the kamikaze or the know all, they can affect confidence for the group and need extra love and attention from the training manager to bring them into the safe zone. I have found that rabbits, much like the animal version, often thrive and multiply in their local area.

The Militant

The final species is the "militant" who is a special version of the kamikaze model with negativity as standard equipment, but with noisy controversial sounds regularly emanating from every orifice.

The militant tries to get others to join their gang and is under the impression that, once unified, they will get something for free from the franchisor. It has to be questioned why they have joined such a constrictive venture and how the franchisor has allowed them to then infiltrate the group. The training manager will spot the militant early and again a quiet chat is often the best option, without compromise I will add.

There are other species but these are the four main ones and the tongue-in-cheek appraisal should be taken with a pinch of salt. It is no different from a group of co-workers and if you have worked in a business with more than three employees there's a very good chance that you have already seen a version of one or more of the species.

Whoever your classmates are, the important thing to remember is that you are there for you, not other classmates, and you should get the most out of the opportunity to learn.

Another piece of advice is to treat the training course as a one-off opportunity to get as much information as you can in a short period of time. The retention of facts does not improve by staying up late every night nibbling peanuts at the bar whilst consuming most of the contents of the hotel cellar. Relax, enjoy but don't overdo it, especially if your alcohol tolerance is minimal.

Watch out for the disruptive types and remain focused on your business and the information on offer to help you succeed.

Where is my bible? – Understanding the operations manual

People within the franchise industry often refer to the "Operations Manual" as the bible. This loose analogy is fairly accurate as it defines the way things have been done, albeit like the bible it was written according to a select few men of faith, in this case the franchisor's team.

Any training course will use the operations manual as a reference to the sessions included in the agenda and will have tutorial sessions covering the main parts of the manual.

A good operation manual is concise and easy to read, with salient points and cross references to what to do and when to do it. Don't expect to read every word during a training course though.

The manual is an ever changing tool that evolves over time, with updates added regularly. For example, when new technology is available to franchisees, new systems are introduced or new techniques developed.

When you receive your manual it is normal to sign a receipt for it and this will state that it remains the property of the franchisor and must not be copied or shared with anyone outside of your business operation. There is also a clause for the return of the manual should you leave the network.

Every manual is different but the format is fairly generic and includes contact information, some history about the company, as well as the procedures for administration functions and reporting.

The control of a system is very important and therefore if you are required to report a certain way then you will have to do it, even if you have an alternative way that works for you. This may seem harsh but if the system breaks down due to everyone becoming a clone of Frank Sinatra doing it "My Way" then confusion may put others in the network at risk. This may seem dramatic but I have seen short cuts cost people their business and life-time savings, so I always maintain a firm line that if you have bought into a system then follow it, otherwise why not start up on your own?

After you have been in business for a while and done exactly what is suggested in the standard blueprint way then you will earn the right to suggest improvements for the collective, and any good franchisor will welcome constructive input.

Treat the Operations Manual as your reference book to business life. As with any reference book you don't need to read every word but use the sections relative to a particular question.

A manual may be a few select pages or a set of volumes, depending on the franchise. There is no definitive manual size and as long as it covers all of the daily activities that you will soon be doing then it is now your bible.

Getting your hands dirty – Classroom versus field training

Although incredibly important and in most cases an effective way of teaching you as a new franchisee, the fact remains that most people want to get out of the classroom and get their hands dirty.

Depending on the franchise, the practical training can form most of the course or very little. For example, a cost reduction franchise will have practice or role play sessions but will be paper orientated. Compare this to a chemical based franchise like ChemEx in which some of the time is spent using the valeting products on a car or in a local kitchen area to clean the ovens, floor and walls.

If your business is a manufacturing concept then the vast majority of the training hours will cover the basic techniques, with one-to-one post-training emphasis with another franchisee or someone from the support team in the franchisee's new store on their territory.

Over the years running training courses I have maintained the philosophy that it is best to keep everything simple: what your product does and what that means to the buyer. Using jargon and "telling" instead of "selling" is basically waffle, and none of us likes waffle. This is another reason why I don't wish to insult you as the reader and waffle for twenty pages about selling techniques. Finding your level, practising the introduction to yourself and engaging in a conversation is the crux of selling.

Think of the introduction the same as you would if you walked into a party. Say who you are and why you are there, who you know and who invited you. After that, conversation starts and you start selling yourself.

A balanced training course will include short theory sessions and a sprinkle of hands-on practical experience. The difficulty is that not every attendee will appreciate every session, fact. People operate in comfort zones and so the former accountant will no doubt love the administration sessions whereas perhaps the former engineer will prefer the practical session.

Induction training is an introduction and the real training starts on the first day in your area. Enjoy the course.

Eager to go – Am I ready?

If the franchisor has done an excellent job then at the end of your induction course you will be highly motivated, full of new knowledge and eager to get started and get earning money from your new venture.

How exciting! A new chapter in your life has started and the world, or at least the territory, should get ready for you, the future Franchisee of the Year.

Even if you feel apprehensive, which is completely normal by the way, the experience of the whole training course will show you that you are not alone. Other franchisees and support staff want to see you succeed and you are very much part of a family now.

Of course you are ready, as ready as you will ever be, and the closing comments will reflect that. I always finished a course with some words of caution that everyone should take their time, do the same thing every day and shout if they needed help. I also used a phrase inherited from Les Gray, founder of ChemEx: "everyone leaves today with the same opportunity and the same level of knowledge, what you do with it is down to you." How true, and an excellent way to end a chapter on training.

Everyone leaves an induction training course with the same opportunity and same level of knowledge, what they do with them is down to them.

6

Make or Break
The First Six Months

I need to make this work – I am going to make this work!

Hello I'm here – Day one, let's start trading

In most cases the end of the induction training course means a weekend at home, or it may be a day or two travelling home from an overseas course.

After you put the key in the door lock and cross the threshold there's a very good chance that you will feel very motivated, eager to get started and earn your first million.

Family and friends will have a lot of questions for you after a long week, or even weeks, in the classroom.

The next few days are the start of a new chapter in your life, but for the moment it is unwritten even if you have the layout of the chapter.

What your first real day is like depends entirely on what your new business offers: whether it is a product or a service, whether customers will have to come to you, or whether you have to go and find customers at their premises. If the business is premises orientated, hopefully the first day is opening day and the franchisor has coordinated launch day for the Monday after the end of induction training. If it a home-based business or one where you need to venture out into the big world, then again Monday may be launch day.

Whichever business you start the franchisor should be there to hold your hand for the first few days.

Allow me to draw a picture of two very different franchise businesses just to show you how different the first days can be.

A Mobile Sales Van Franchise

ChemEx franchisees had a business development manager with them first thing Monday morning to go over the van stock, before announcing that it was "time to hit the road and knock on some doors."

The challenge was then on to take a franchisee to potential new customers, cold calling in essence, and to make a sale for them on the first day. The philosophy was that if you didn't show them you could do it then how could you expect them to do it? When a new starter had an existing business we still took them cold calling for the first day but with a full customer list to hand so we didn't inadvertently barge into an existing customer before the handover scheduled with the outgoing franchisee.

Tuesday was a confidence building day and after a couple of calls the business manager would stand back and let the franchisee start selling. It didn't matter if mistakes were made as it was part of the training process with constructive advice, not criticism, used to hone the franchisee's skills. This was seen as an ongoing process, which is why there was a twelve-week development programme with at least a day a week with a development manager, culminating in a review course back in the classroom.

Retail Based Franchise

Signarama, on the other hand, is a store-based business and over a two-week period the support team would help recruit and train the new production and sales employees while the owner prepared for launch by introducing the products to local businesses and providing a quote here and there with a member of the support team.

The support continued in the second week, which was usually the official launch date. Members of the Signarama team continued to nurture the employees and the owner with a clear objective: to get lots of quotes done which would inevitably turn into business and sales revenue. The fully trained production team also had a member of the support team to produce the orders gained from the sales activity.

After this initial two-week intensive launch process the support team attended for at least a day a week and made daily contact with the franchisee in the first few months.

Just two examples and by no way definitive for home-based or premises-based businesses. There are hundreds of franchises available and each has a version that offers support in its own way.

Be patient, building a business takes time and effort. Despite your enthusiasm remember that every potential customer that you approach is not a guaranteed sale, they have not been sitting around waiting for you to start your business with an open cheque book, pen poised!

Brick walls – Overcoming the fear of failure

If anyone tells you that they have never hit a brick wall in their business then they are lying. It may be a little wall easily stepped over, or a fortified position preventing you from achieving your goal. Sometimes the wall gets bigger as you approach it, with a moat and defenders ready to repel invaders, in fact it appears an impenetrable obstacle; however walls can be scaled, bypassed or smashed and destroyed.

It is also true is that getting past or around a brick wall is easier with people to help you overcome the obstacle. This, if anything, is the essence of franchising.

Most of us fear failure and get scared at some time in our personal or working life. Often the way that we overcome the fear is to turn away from the problem and in turn the fear itself. Of course this isn't overcoming the fear; it is ignoring and avoiding the problem that is still there.

Isn't it better to address the fear, challenge the problem? Instead of thinking of the ramifications of not achieving a goal by letting the wall stop you, why not think of the ramifications of failing to find a solution or a way past the wall?

The Sales Wall

If sales are low then surely it is better to work harder at getting new customers, sell more to existing customers or thinking of ways to improve your sales technique. Speaking with others who may have had the same problems in a franchise network, as well as the franchisor's support staff, is a good way to get advice.

The biggest brick wall in most franchises is a lack of sales. The problem is that people make it complicated and think of it as the science of sales. I don't think that the science of selling is that difficult to teach to anyone and despite the plethora of sales guides from the gurus, the simple fact remains that to sell to someone you need to be "you" and then at some point in a conversation *ask for the order*.

As I mentioned in the last chapter, selling is in essence about having a comfortable conversation with someone and listening.

The Solo Wall

No, this section is nothing to do with Star Wars, although Jedi mind tricks may be part of the problem. Believe it or not, some people have a real problem changing from employees to self-employed business people. Time and support from the franchisor is the way of overcoming this obstacle and often the support manager will adopt a dictatorial approach initially, regularly checking up on the franchisee and giving ideas and action points. Over time the franchise manager will wean the franchisee off the daily task list until all of a sudden they are less reliant and more self sufficient.

The Garden Wall

Problems at home, often born out of the dramatic lifestyle change, are another brick wall that franchisees confront. This is why it is a very good idea, if not essential, that a franchisee's life partner is involved in the meeting process before signing up and is also made aware of the implications. A good franchisor will offer assistance, sitting down with the couple and listening to the grievances in an attempt to reassure the partner. Thereafter a commitment for additional support is often made to help the franchisee work through the problems at home by delivering success in the business. Remember that this is a partnership within a partnership and the franchisor wants to help and have happy franchisees.

Wall Street

The final common brick wall is nothing to do with the New York financial district but loosely to do with finances.

Financing any business comes with headaches and these can turn into migraines if the financial records and control are poorly maintained. The franchisee sees a huge wall that seems to have appeared form nowhere but corresponds with an overdraft limit reached or the savings plundered. The annoying thing is that the business levels are usually good and it is a simple case of getting money in more quickly from customers. If this is the case the wall will disappear with a little more effort at collecting cash. This is a simple solution but surprisingly, the most common mistake that franchisees make is credit control, or a lack of it.

Maintaining good financial records requires discipline, which might mean allocating a day every week to administration tasks such as accounts. Contacting customers about payments due is also a great way of ensuring that you maximise potential sales by taking an interest in their stock levels or finding out whether they have carried out an action recommended from the service that you offer.

Occasionally the financial wall is because sales are low and costs have drained financial resources. If this is the case then the best advice is to let the franchisor know there is a possible problem so that they can work with you to secure additional finance or address your particular circumstances sooner rather than later.

Sometimes all that you need is a boost of self confidence from someone who also keeps it simple. Asking for advice is the way that you start to overcome your fear of failure. After that, if you need some extra tuition in a particular area then you will be better equipped to break the wall down.

Walls get in the way of every business but they can be breached if you work with the franchisor on solid action plans.

But I have tried that – Keep doing what you have been taught

People often build their own walls. The sad fact is that they don't follow the programme and "pigeon hole" types of customers from a negative experience. I have lost count of the times a franchisee has told me that a certain type of customer isn't interested in "us", with excuses such as the products are not used or we are too expensive. This is sometimes difficult to understand or accept when a neighbouring franchisee has a dozen or so customers in the same business and sells at a good margin. The truth is often that they have seen one or two prospects and not gained a sale and so, by definition, everyone in that business is a non-starter.

All salespeople get lazy over time and forget a step of the sale, maybe a poor introduction, or ignoring the golden rule which is to listen to what people say – telling instead of selling.

Building a business is a gradual process and it relies on building relationships, getting referrals and reviewing the progress with support managers. The following sections should expand on these key areas by providing you with some interesting nuggets of information.

My Customers – Building relationships

A good customer should ideally be a friend or acquaintance, someone who enjoys your company even if you take money off them for the service provided or product sold.

Building relationships relies on good "people skills": being able to communicate about subjects outside of the business, such as a customer's home life or family. For many people this is second nature, however some need to develop their people skills in a natural way so as not to appear sycophantic!

Taking an interest in someone personally instead of discussing work every time is really quite a simple process and is an extension of questioning techniques that people use in sales presentations, but with an emphasis on conversation rather than obvious commercial questions. Using your eyes is the key when you visit a customer; look for the plaque on the wall, coffee cup with a favourite team or "The World's Best Dad", or simply a photo frame on a desk. Just think of the standard questions hairdressers use while they snip and colour hair. Bring home life into a conversation and then make a note or remember if something is due to happen. The next time you visit ask how it went, for example the graduation of their child, or a holiday, a wedding, sporting event or a house move.

Getting the customer to relax enough to discuss personal events takes time and is often part of questioning techniques.

This may seem intrusive but if a customer volunteers information during a conversation then don't ignore it: use it, show an interest, and build a relationship.

Apart from the personal part of building relationships it is very important to deliver products or services on time and in full. Excellent customer service boosts the relationship potential whilst protecting sales revenue.

Nugget... in a Nutshell

Building relationships with customers not only secures a good working relationship but can help protect business if a competitor tries to take the business from you.

Who else – The importance of referrals

What is a referral? No matter what the definition, the referral is one of the strongest tools available to a business person. Asking a satisfied customer if they know of anyone who might benefit from your products or services may seem cheeky but it is a question that may get you another customer.

The key to getting referrals is asking every customer this question at least once. The timing of the referral question is normally after you have delivered the service sold to that customer, not during the first sales call.

Offering an incentive to a customer, such as a monthly draw for a meal for two, or a voucher, can boost the referrals gained. The key to any reward system is to remember to say thank you while giving the person who gave you the referral something for nothing.

If someone does give you a referral then make sure that you ask if it is alright to use their name and that you contact the referral quickly. This may seem a little dramatic but think how you would feel if someone asked you for a name of a friend and then a month later you bumped into that person and asked how they got on with the business person only to hear that they hadn't even bothered to call your friend.

Referrals are a fantastic sales tool. Remember to ask every satisfied customer if they know of anyone else who might benefit from the products or service that you offer. This might be a friend or family member who is also in business.

How am I doing? – Business reviews and honest views

A good franchisor will keep in touch with you regularly during the embryonic stage of your business, the first six months or so.

Business reviews may seem very formal but they are an integral part of the support function and require open discussion of progress made and planned activity going forward.

Beware of the sales rut, which is very common. You start your business and do exactly what the programme states for the first three months, only to wonder why the business plateaus at six months. The usual reason is that franchisees think that it is easy when sales start to come in from customers seen three months ago and so they ease off, only to experience a plateau in revenue three months later. Keep doing the same thing every day for at least the first year and I guarantee that the sales will increase if you follow the successful programme. Franchisees often miss this point but it is fundamental to the success of your business.

A business review is an opportunity to review negative points as well and flag where additional training is required. Keeping an open mind to suggestions is very important, especially when additional training will benefit your business and these suggestions are accepted as constructive criticism.

Attend business reviews with an open mind and accept that the advice offered is geared to improving your business turnover and operational activity.

Starting to build – Hitting break-even and aiming high

Overcoming obstacles, building relationships with customers, getting referrals and being honest in appraising your progress is the recipe for success.

The first important figure is the break-even target, which is usually the sales figure required to cover stock cost and direct overheads like rent or lease costs. Everything above this figure is potential profit or earnings for a franchisee.

The danger in analysing break-even is that although you achieve the golden figure in, for example, month six, the previous five months will, by definition, have accrued losses. So what is the true break-even figure? The business break-even is surely when the total sales exceed the total costs since the business started trading; this is going to be achieved by regularly exceeding the monthly break-even figure, which is why franchisors often concentrate on this golden figure in isolation and congratulate you on achieving it.

Understand the ongoing trading break-even figure is not just a stand-alone monthly break-even value – remember that continual over-achievement of the stand-alone figure will eventually cover the losses built up and repay your investment.

Once you have achieved the regular break-even figure it is easier to visualise what you need to do to hit higher targets. This may mean investment in additional employees or equipment, but at least you will be able to make a decision with knowledge and a track record of regular growth and profits achieved during your first six months.

7

Here to Stay

Getting Past the First Year

I'm getting into this – now let's build a solid business!

Expanding possibilities – Investing in growth

The first six months are the crucial time for any business. Taking your foot off the accelerator is the biggest mistake that new businesses make. People stop doing what brought them success and they don't see the impact until a few months after that.

Nobody expects to be a millionaire after a few short months but building the foundations in the first twelve months is important if you want a business for the rest of your life, or until you decide to sell and reap the rewards.

Any good franchisor will want to see you succeed and deliver exceptional growth, with the ulterior motive that they will maximise their licence fees and any other income streams associated with your operation. The second benefit is that it makes it easier to attract new franchisees and roll out the programme in the country and overseas. It is important to note that franchisors may suggest you invest in expansion into new areas or hire additional staff to maximise their own income stream, but diverting profits into investment will have an impact on your earnings and the family income. The franchisor will use the carrot of the financial reward from doubling, trebling, or quadrupling of a second, third and even a fourth profitable business unit. Sometimes this vision is the right choice but be cautious, as sometimes the increased overhead and division of your time could prove crippling and the whole business may suffer beyond repair.

With this cautionary note, the positive message is that you must take the fundamental risks of investment and expansion if you do want to realise the maximum potential for any given area or location, but you might be happier with the initial business and the income you derive from it.

This decision is sometimes taken away from you if the franchisor operates undefined areas and has the option to open another franchise within spitting distance if you refuse to open another outlet. This option is rare but is used by quite a few franchise brands, in particular some fast food outlets, to ensure maximum brand awareness and blanket coverage. Your lawyer will no doubt have mentioned this when reviewing the contract, as mentioned in Chapter Two.

The good thing is that most franchisors don't charge you a second fee when you expand to a second retail outlet, vehicle or industrial unit if you have a defined territory. The investment is therefore pure investment in your business.

Investment comes in many forms. Opening a new unit may involve a lease deposit and the legal fees associated. Shop fitting, signage or staff training are the normal additional costs to consider. The investment may be another vehicle, as well as the employee who will drive it, if the franchise is van based, along with the equipment needed. This may be a small investment compared to a new ten-year lease on a building; however the impact is another salary, fuel and hope that the employee can deliver in the role to make the investment work.

Be aware before you expand your business that finding the right employees is not always easy. You may have to consider that some may not work as hard or as well as you do and you will need to adopt a new role as a people manager, with added patience!

Whatever investment or expansion options are available, it is wise to go back a few pages in this book and research the cost and impact in exactly the same way that you did before deciding to start your journey as a franchisee.

If the planning and research has been done properly then the decision is easy.

Even if your business is "flying" in the first year it is important to take time before making any decision to expand – make sure you understand the financial impact and risk to your income and the impact on family finances.

I want more – Surpassing your targets

Targets are fabulous, for most people! Deciding on a realistic target is normally a joint decision between the franchisee and franchisor. Occasionally a franchise agreement includes a contractual target that you have to achieve, although it is usually a low figure.

Of course the franchisor may have challenged you to over-achieve the minimum mediocre figures and be the prime candidate for a "Franchisee of the Year" award.

Psychology works both ways when considering targets: if you don't achieve then you may become de-motivated, whereas over-achieving may spur you on to even greater success. I have always believed that targets are fabulous, however the real benefit of targets for employed sales teams or individual franchisees is that they should be moveable, to maximise the motivation of the individual.

I resisted the temptation to add a detailed example of a franchisee initially missing the target but catching up. The process is far too complex to explain in words, and a tad boring for you to read. Instead the message is simple; if you are behind a target don't worry, because there is every chance that you can catch up with a bumper month! Use a simple calculation based on the last three months sales, multiply this value by four and you have a fairly accurate run rate. Next month do the same and as long as it is a higher value your business is growing.

I have concentrated on sales targets because this is what most companies use every day, and therefore so should you.

But don't forget!

I totally appreciate that variable considerations apply as well and if you sell a product at a reduced margin then you need more sales to make up the lost profit, which in turn affects the contribution to the fixed costs. If you have £2,000 per month fixed costs for the rent or lease and you make 100% profit on everything you sell, then in simple terms every £1,000 of sales brings in £500 profit, so to cover the £2,000 as well you need to sell £4,000 every month. Using the simple calculation, let us assume that you need to take £2,000 a month personally. A target of at least £5,000 of extra sales will deliver this bare minimum, with a little extra to cover variable costs and even a contribution to future taxes.

Of course you probably want more, so setting a target of £10,000 for three months, increasing by another £1,000 a month, is very sensible.

Motivate the team – Incentives

If you employ staff then everyone plays a part in achieving a target and so it makes sense to increase the team effort by using incentives to really help you reach and surpass targets.

It is important to make sure that incentives are rolling and that employees don't work the system by delivering exceptional results one month, taking a bonus and then under-achieving the next before again delivering dramatic results, and so on. Be aware of the loopholes and make sure that part of any incentive includes a rolling evaluation for maximum benefit.

Remain focused when setting targets and only set achievable values based on your new found knowledge as a franchisee. Grow your business sensibly and remember that a gradual growth rate is much better than boom and bust targets. Adopting this "real" approach will help you build a business that can then look after you for the rest of your life!

Don't be afraid to ask – Ongoing support from your franchisor

During the first year you will inevitably develop your own methods that may vary slightly from the bible version contained in the operation manual. I have mentioned previously that it is dangerous to change anything and that you should follow the system to the letter for the first twelve months; but I am not that naïve! There will be some methods that you will always change to suit your individual style and relative experience.

This is fine as long as you have achieved your target; if not and you need more help, then shout for support. Do it sooner rather than later, without waiting to be asked if you need it.

You might be unaware that you have started to develop bad habits because they have not affected your business, but if retained they might damage you next year.

Excellent forums for both new and established franchisees are regional meetings and national conventions. Most good franchisors get franchisees together regularly. I inherited a solid system at ChemEx from my peers who understood the importance of communication, and continued with meetings three times a year, or twice when a national conference appeared on the calendar.

These meetings were planned well in advance and meant that I would set off up the M6 motorway to Scotland on a Sunday morning for the first meeting either later that day or first thing Monday. The regional support team then traversed the country from north to south, calling at another eight venues. I digress, but the feedback gained was invaluable and, more importantly for this section of the book, it allowed people to ask questions and seek advice from not only the gamekeepers but the other poachers.

If someone was having a difficult time it wasn't unusual for an experienced franchisee to offer a day or two to help the struggling rookie and show him how the old timer did it.

National – or even international – conventions bring everyone together and also offer rookies a sense of belonging to the bigger family. Due to the nature of these well planned events the transfer of ideas and support from other franchisees is usually confined to the network sessions or splinter seminars set up as part of the overall agenda and perceived glitzy stage presentations from key executives and key note speakers drafted in to offer external motivation speeches.

Whatever the gathering, be it regional, national or international, it provides rookies with another chance to ask for help from others, not just the franchisor.

The franchisor is your business partner so ask for help and guidance if you need it. Nothing is gained from burying your head and keeping problems to yourself. Attend regional and national meetings and talk to successful franchisees for tips and nuggets that can improve how you work. Remember that everyone wants you to succeed.

Have I done as much as I could have? – Reflecting on the first twelve months

Self assessment is a very important part of being in business and is fine as long as you are pragmatic in your approach.

Be honest with yourself and ask the question "have I done everything that I was taught and, more importantly, done everything I could have, every day, meticulously?" If the answer is "no" there may be reasons and as long as they are valid reasons then they form part of the appraisal. But if the reasons are merely excuses then perhaps you should learn from them and make sure they do not hamper your chances in the future. Self assessment requires you to use the exercise as a valuable tool in assessing where you can improve or where you need to focus.

Even those who have achieved targets can self assess and see how they can improve and over-achieve.

If you have done most of what you could and followed the system, there is no reason why your business should not be profitable and successful at the end of the first year, with a solid foundation to build a great business for you and your family for many years to come.

Work hard, but more importantly work smart and make sure that you keep doing the same things every day for the first twelve months. Look at yourself in the mirror and ask whether you have done everything possible to turn your venture into a successful business – be honest when you ask this question.

8

When the Time is Right

Planning Your Exit

Cash the chips in or pass it on!

Roll up, roll up – Marketing your business

Don't worry: you have not missed a chapter, the printers didn't miss some pages in the binding process and I didn't forget something when reading over the manuscript again and again.

The fact is that whatever takes place between finishing training and the day that you sell your business is unique to you, therefore to try to explain what to do, aside from the advice already given, would only be adding words to the same message under a different title or section.

Darwin penned "Origin of the Species" over many years, eventually publishing it in 1859. It documented the evolution of man and other inhabitants of this world and their ability to adapt to the environment. In some ways franchising as an environment has required individuals to adapt and evolve. Individual franchisees have bonded together in groups within franchise companies and grown stronger collectively.

Wait! Isn't this is a little deep? Perhaps not, as the analogy does fit. Through natural selection weaker franchisees leave and are replaced by others who use knowledge and experience to adapt and succeed. Stronger franchisees provide feedback for others joining the network and thus the franchise evolves as a group within a global market.

As with all groups, packs or other collective noun for a number of like-minded individuals, there comes a time when some leave the group and venture off to greener pastures.

The action of moving on has an effect on those you leave behind and the franchise family supports the collective. The person leaving also severs the ties that supported them as a part of the group, so there is a psychological impact on more than one individual.

Deciding to sell

Often the decision to sell is reactionary but it doesn't have to be; planning your exit well in advance is a great idea that you should discuss with the franchisor so they can help you start planning early. I have sat down with franchisees and talked to them about exit plans sometimes three years in the future.

The decision to sell is very much down to timing and personal circumstances. Remember that in most cases it requires discussion with the franchisor, who has the final say in accepting a suitable buyer.

If you do decide to sell then it may take some time unless a suitable candidate happens to be talking to the recruitment team already.

It is not unusual for a franchisor to try to convince you to change your mind, especially if you have a successful business that they refer to as part of the recruitment process. Franchisors don't like to lose good franchisees who deliver sales and provide income. The disruption of a new franchisee in an area can affect the income stream for the franchisor and in some cases start a chain reaction for other successful franchisees to consider selling as well.

The Process

The nuts and bolts of selling a business are similar from franchise to franchise. Most franchise sales are handled by the franchisor that will seek a suitable buyer from the ongoing lead generation underway for new franchisees. At any time it is not unusual for 10–20% of any established network to be seeking a buyer if the exit price is right.

When I first started working in this glorious industry I was shocked that one in five franchises may be up for sale but soon realised that this churn was actually healthy, with new blood further developing territories.

What is interesting is that franchisors used to treat the resale subject as a taboo item, never admitting to having as many franchises up for sale. It was quite funny at franchise exhibitions with everyone denying that they had anyone up for sale. Everyone was happy and recruitment was the highest ever! True for some but a little white lie for most.

Thankfully this attitude changed and active marketing of areas for sale began during the early part of the new millennium. This sea change actually brought the industry in line with all other type of business sales and made it easier to discuss the reasons why people wanted to sell, as they were no different from any other business.

Some franchise-specific web portals created resale-specific pages for the marketing of franchise businesses. The information often includes current turnover and profit, to attract interest.

A Little Extra Help

It is not unusual for some franchisees to consider additional marketing options straightaway, if they want a quick sale.

There are a variety of options to broaden the exposure of their business. Franchisor approval is usually needed prior to a franchisee opting for this additional exposure and this approval is often given only after an initial period when the normal recruitment process has already been tried. There are a number of ways to market outside of the franchise specific avenue. The examples are not an exhaustive list, as new and exciting ways seem to pop up every month, all designed to obtain advertising fees or even a slice of the selling price.

Weekly newspapers, such as Daltons, offer many types of businesses for sale, including the occasional franchise-specific section. Newspapers may seem old fashioned and "yesterday's news, today's fish and chips wrapper", but that was twenty years ago, before hygiene concerns saw the end of chips stuck to the racing results from Aintree. For many the printed word is still the preferred way of finding out what is available.

Numerous web portals and business agents will find a buyer, for a percentage or just a fixed fee. Be careful if you consider this route as they don't realise the need and condition for the franchisor to approve and accept a buyer under the agreement. It is not unusual for these agents to try to get you to drop the franchise connection to make it easier for you to sell, but that is just not a good policy.

Keeping it in the Family

Selling to a neighbouring franchisee that wants to expand may be an option, but again this is subject to approval from the franchisor.

Normal activity is usually enough for a successful franchise to attract a buyer, if you have the time and patience to let the marketing work, but if you want a quick fire sale to get out then discussing other options early is probably the best route. However, you should expect to sell at a lower price and with additional cost, which brings me onto the next subject.

Nugget... in a Nutshell

Keep your options open and, much the same as selling a house, you should get regular updates from the franchisor. Remember that someone buying a franchise business has to consider the benefit of joining a network as well, so it can take longer to sell a franchised business compared to a non- franchised business – be patient!

It will cost you this much – Valuing your business

It is important to note that selling a business is not always easy, especially if the value is out of kilter in your mind's eye compared to the real value.

Whether you are selling after developing an area or after a short while there is a perceived value for your effort, no matter what the level of turnover you achieved. Unfortunately this is often an inflated value and is not dissimilar to selling a house after spending time, money and effort fitting a new kitchen, bathroom or conservatory. The reality is that the location really defines the value and even if you have spent thousands it does not equate to another 20% on the base value of similar bricks and mortar in the road, avenue or close. The luxury additions may help you sell more quickly and you can achieve a premium if the buyer acknowledges that there is added value.

If you are selling the equivalent of a bulk standard semi-detached house without any nice extras then don't expect to sell for a premium. The buyer will have to pay legal fees and stamp duty for a house, and for a franchise there are training courses, initial stock and set-up package costs. For example, if you buy a virgin area franchise for £22,000, which is defined in the agreement as £10,000 for the area and £12,000 for training, then a new franchisee buying your business will have to pay £12,000 for their training so the base value is £10,000. If you have zero or low sales and want to sell the business then all you can expect to recoup from a sale is £10,000, not the £22,000 you paid.

I have used this example for many years and it may seem a little drastic, but it is similar to the different values for someone who has developed a business that is at or around break-even point and it seems fair in real terms to me.

From the franchisor's perspective, a possible buyer has a mixture of positive and negative reactions to an area with a break-even figure.

Positive first: a buyer gets a business that should take less time to build, if it is a repeat order business. Negative second: a logical question is "why has the current franchisee only built the business to a paltry level?" Ah, the difficult question that may have a number of legitimate answers, such as ill health, lack of sales activity, or even that the owner only worked the business part time.

Whatever the reason, the role of the franchisor is critical in the sale.

Marketing the business at the right price is the first consideration. Agreeing the value with the franchisor is imperative.

Thankfully, most franchise agreements set out the costs involved when selling a business and the contribution towards the process required from both parties.

Selling businesses is a complex subject and involves the same basic ideals, whether the sale is for £20,000 or £20 million. The value is derived from one of a number of valuation calculations using turnover, profit or future value as the benchmark, with a multiple of the benchmark to derive a value.

Most franchise companies use turnover as the easiest benchmark with a brand new virgin area franchise, without any sales at all. In simple terms, this is the stated cost of a franchise.

Any franchise for sale with turnover up to the break-even figures used in the profit examples is probably the same price as a virgin area. There might be an argument here for a small premium but if the business is not generating profit it is difficult to sell to a potential buyer.

A franchise for sale with turnover over the break-even figure should derive a premium. This premium varies considerably and your franchisor will use a number of considerations. To avoid pages of waffle, it is best to discuss this at the right time with your franchisor.

It is fairly common to use a turnover-based valuation of the total turnover, so someone with £36,000 turnover has a business valued at £36,000.

You also have to consider how much a bank will lend to a potential buyer of your franchise. The bank will want to see your accounts as well to ascertain its profitability.

Ideally a bank will want to see three years of accounts, although in franchising this is not always available if the franchisee sells after two years. Another point to mention is that if you have built your business from a virgin area then the first year's profit will be lower and therefore your current valuation, based on the last year's higher profits, may be higher than the average that the bank may use for its own lending criteria. Most banks will only lend up to three times the net profit, so if your valuation is say five times the net profit the bank may not lend your prospective buyer the full value and they will have to fund the remainder from personal cash and equities. The bank will also want to ensure that loan repayments are covered by at least twice the current net profit. For example, if the loan repayments are £12,000 then the net profit needs to be at least £24,000.

Don't forget that the buyer will have considered the implications of buying a business in exactly the same way as you did when you first looked at starting a franchise business, as mentioned in Chapter Three. They still need to understand the risks associated with borrowing money from the banks and the need for security to guarantee the borrowing.

More Complex Valuations

If a franchisor uses an analytical approach to consider profit, break-even and margin, the valuation relies on a formula approach.

Let us assume that a virgin area is valued at £22,000 and you have a turnover of £66,000 when you decide to sell. If the margin is 50% then £33,000 gross profit is generated with a break-even of say £20,000 to cover fixed costs, therefore £13,000 net profit.

Are you still with me? Good. With a tangible profit to play with, plus the effective area fee, you would expect to recoup £10,000 plus, say, a multiple of twice the profit. The value would therefore be in the region of £36,000.

The buyer would pay this amount and the franchisor would then deduct the training costs, plus any contractual commission.

Let us assume £12,000 for training plus 5% of the sale value, which is another £1,800, therefore £13,800 total.

The net proceeds are, for this basic example, £36,000 less £13,800, therefore £22,200.

Faced with this apparently low figure, remember that you have had the training and set-up package, which the buyer as a new franchisee requires as well.

As a good payout relies on better turnover and profit, a turnover of £132,000 would give you £66,000 profit. Using the same basic calculation, this would be £46,000 net profit after deducting the fixed costs. Twice the profit plus the £10,000 area fee equates to a sale value of £102,000; after taking off the 5% and training costs this would give you net proceeds of £84,900, nearly four times your initial investment and a good return.

Other Valuation Methods

Some franchisors use a multiple of the profit as a valuation technique so that the net profit is usually multiplied by two, three or more to get a value. Using the basic examples above and say two and a half times the profit as the multiple, the lower £66,000 turnover would give a value of £32,500 and the higher turnover of £132,000 a value of £115,000 - values similar to the complex calculation in the last section.

The most difficult method is "future value" and is normally used when a business has a unique product or contracts that will derive growth in future years. This type of sale is usually confined to larger organisations and although many franchises use future values and potential as the mainstay of sales presentations, the use in valuation terms is dodgy.

Although this section may seem a little longwinded it is important to understand how businesses are valued, especially when a franchisor might dictate the method without much explanation.

What is abundantly clear from the previous pages is that the most important factor, aside the valuation method, is the turnover and therefore the profits your business generates at the time of selling.

When you sell a franchised business it usually involves the purchaser taking over stock and equipment and any leases that are still running, so an asset sale is the usual method with the valuation derived from net profit. Share valuations are based on profit ratios while asset valuations include tangible assets as well as profit generated. The best person to speak to about the valuation is your franchise manager. Most potential purchasers are looking for the opportunity to run a business, generate a good income for a number of years and then sell the business with a premium value, whether it is a franchise or independent non-franchise operation.

Whatever valuation method a franchisor uses the value of your business relies on maintaining business levels right up to transferring the business. Valuations can go down if you lose business turnover between the valuation process and signing the handover.

Over to you – The franchisor's role in the sale

I have already hinted that the franchisor has a big role in the sale scenario and eventually the approval of any sale rests solely with the franchisor, with consideration to the suitability of a buyer as a new franchisee.

I would hazard a guess that over 90% of resale transactions are secured by the franchisor from the ongoing marketing of the business to a wider audience. This leaves 10% from direct specific marketing of a particular or a number of resale opportunities.

The normal process that franchisors use is to interview potential franchisees and when there is a real interest in a virgin territory they introduce a new angle: a potential opportunity of a resale with the added benefit of a quantifiable turnover. This may be a business that is available at a slightly higher price. The benefit of an almost guaranteed turnover is certainly worth considering, especially if the valuation is not far off a virgin territory price.

The same approach is often used for higher turnover opportunities, with an established business introduced to suitable and well financed individuals at the appropriate time.

The ticket price of an established business with considerable turnover is going to be much higher, therefore the negotiation needs to be much more sensitive so that the incumbent operator is not compromised in any way.

Over the years I have seen a lack of discretion by franchisees selling established businesses. Their loose tongues allowed competitors to capitalise just by touting for business and letting prospective customers know that the franchisee would be moving on. In one case, a particular franchisee lost his top three customers and in turn 30% of his turnover, which had a considerable effect on the resale value. Ouch! This is because he tried to get a competitor to buy his business as a quick option. Lesson learned for all who follow.

Any good franchisor will position any potential resale opportunity at the second or even third meeting, unless someone attends the interview based on an advertised resale, of course.

Even if someone does apply via a specific resale advertisement, the same selection and interview techniques will be followed to ascertain whether the individual is suitable and a good fit for the particular franchise.

The franchisor will discuss the value of the area, which reinforces the need for common ground on any valuation at the outset. He will also explain, if not sell, the training costs and set-up costs.

If everyone is happy with the detail then the sale will proceed, subject to the incoming buyer passing the training course and the handover being completed in a timely manner.

Let the franchisor handle the sale of your business and watch what you say to everyone – It is better to keep a sale close to your chest until a deal is done. This includes telling fellow franchisees and your customers

Here are the keys – The handover of the business

In the commercial world businesses are bought and sold every day and in most cases there are conditions to protect the vendor and buyer to ensure full agreed payment, subject to a true valuation.

The difference in franchising, per se, is that due diligence is not normally carried out because the franchisor should have a monitoring process in place, which verifies the sales turnover and compliance with an agreement that is in force. A franchisee would not declare ghost sales figures because it would probably cost him higher licence fees and even tax liability. The costs will be standard and easy to verify, especially if the franchisor knows the premises or vehicle lease costs and the amount of stock bought direct or via approved third-party suppliers. In short, as there is very little that could be hidden the buyer has more confidence in the stated figures of a franchise than an independent business.

It is incredibly important for the vendor to maintain the customer base and keep quiet until the handover is about to take place because the sale price may depend on the turnover backed up by a customer list, and the turnover if it is a repeat-order business. If the franchise is not a regular repeat-order business then the customer list may be less important but conversely, the current active quotes or potential business under discussion may be more important.

Whatever the type of business or customer base, the important message here is to have continuity for employees and customers so that business is not lost because the employees feel vulnerable.

Another warning message, especially in a repeat-order business, is to maintain good supply relationships, resisting the temptation to over-sell to customers to get rid of stock at a discount and make a few extra pennies. It happens, but can actually negate a valuation, especially if the buyer picks up on the obvious during a handover. I have seen outgoing franchisees sell twelve months stock at huge discount to gain a few extra pounds, only to lose a sale of their whole business because of the greed factor.

Apart the effect on a sale, the customer may feel compromised as well and use this as an excuse to change suppliers.

The Handover Process

The handover itself largely depends on the type of business and the vendor's need to introduce the buyer to customers. There may be an list of key accounts that the franchisor has agreed with both vendor and buyer and once everyone is content with a suitable handover the buyer will sign a release form that will conclude the sale and release any proceeds to the vendor.

On some occasions the buyer may refuse to sign this document because of an insignificant objection usually in an attempt to get the price down. If this does occur the franchisor usually intervenes very quickly and acts as the arbitrator, with confidence that the sale agreement, signed by the buyer, has a clause stating that they cannot be unreasonable unless a fundamental breach of the contract is found. There may be some brokering required if the reason is something that will impact on the new franchisee's business, for example if the vendor has not maintained the customer base or has been greedy, as mentioned previously.

A simple way for the handover process to go seamlessly is for the vendor and buyer to use the same reason or story when informing customers of the change in ownership. A plausible simple reason is best, even if the real reason may be complex. I am not suggesting fabricating a story for customers, just using the same reason.

When you hand over to a new franchisee keep a record of all joint visits made just in case the new owner disputes that the handover was completed. If a regular customer is not available then it is a good idea to send a letter thanking them for their business and introducing the new owner.

Where's my cheque? – Getting the proceeds

At the end of the handover process the vendor and buyer sign a document with the franchisor, which is sent to the franchisor.

It is reasonable to expect to get a payment quickly as the funds will more than likely be in the franchisor's account already as part of the condition of sale, perhaps in an escrow account if it is a large amount.

It is always a good idea to copy the handover agreement and retain a copy, or even scan the original and email it prior to the hard copy arriving at the franchisor in the post. The acceptance of electronic copies is not normally legally binding therefore a franchisor who doesn't accept an electronic version is not being churlish. Likewise, sending a photocopy without the original penned signature may also delay the process of sending you the money.

There is normally a condition as part of the handover or sale document that payment is due a certain number of days after the handover document is delivered to the franchisor. Today, bank transfers are quicker than the cheque process and provide cleared funds far more quickly than the historic five-day clearance that the banking system dictated.

A good franchisor will ring-fence the proceeds to avoid using the funds but a new franchisor may depend on cash generation to a greater extent and therefore may use the funds inadvertently to aid cash flow.

The "cheque's in the post" excuse is a little obvious and thankfully, with the advent of internet banking, that excuse is almost obsolete.

The reality is that there should be absolutely no reason why the agreed proceeds do not arrive in your nominated bank account within three days of a signed handover, although it may be within a set period. Check the small print on the handover document or even the franchise agreement.

The handover is usually the final part of your contractual liability with the franchise although you will still be bound to the non-compete clauses for a period of time.

The only variance worth mentioning is if there are stage payments agreed as part of the sale process. There might be a covenant on turnover level, although this is very unlikely in franchising because the historic figures are evident and the new franchisee may lose business due to customers going into receivership or because they don't get on with the new franchisee. Almost like a divorce, both sides usually agree to a clean break.

Make sure that you keep copies of all documents sent to the franchisor and let them know that the original copies are on their way

Life after – Something new to do!

Wouldn't it be great to write that every franchisee who has sold then retired? Alas it is not the case. For those who can retire this section is probably irrelevant, but those who may not have that luxury and need to find something from which to derive an income should read on.

Plenty of people buy another franchise and start something new with another company. They might exchange a van-based franchise for a white-collar management franchise, or vice versa.

Moving into a new franchise may seem like shunning the original franchise but this isn't the case. New and exciting franchises emerge every year. Sometimes franchisees switch to a different market in a similar style franchise with a renewed vigour to build another business for profit before selling that one off.

Franchising gets into the blood. Many people like the security and support it offers and so a new concept may be the ideal option, no matter what the reason.

The good thing is that with knowledge and opinion, the decision process outlined is easier the second than the first time.

The experience of running a business under a franchise system will also steer people into independent businesses after they have learnt the fundamental lessons under the controlled system.

For some people, a job and therefore a regular salary is a welcome change after the variable income from running their own business. Going back on the "payroll" is a big decision and one that is fraught with problems after being their own boss since the year "nineteen oatcake." I have seen many ex-franchisees try and fail as employees, only to emerge again as a franchisee with a new concept. Indeed, there have been occasions when people have come back to the comfort zone of the known franchise and have purchased an area without paying a full fee because they don't need full training, only a refresher course.

One final option, which is rare but not unheard of, is setting up a new franchise as a franchisor. Yes it does happen and transferring the knowledge gained as a poacher to the gamekeeper is a natural progression.

This is why this offering exposes both sides in one book, giving invaluable advice to those franchisees who want to set their own concept. On the other hand, seeing what the franchisor has to do and how they run the business will be useful to a franchisee anyway.

If this is as far as you read then I hope that the journey planner has helped you.

Part Two

Taking a Good Concept into Franchising

9

I know, I'll Set up a Franchise

Recognising a Real Franchise Opportunity

Ooh an epiphany – Grow quickly FRANCHISE IT!

Let's convert the company – Franchising an existing business

Most new franchise opportunities evolve from a successful local business; the shareholders want to expand to new locations but have financial constraints on the required capital to invest in premises, resource, stock and vehicles. A few are brand new concepts starting from scratch, and some are imports from successful overseas operations.

I have spoken to plenty of people who have a vision and a desire to convert their little baby into a national and thereafter an international name through franchising, but most don't realise the implications of such a move and, after a little advice, don't proceed.

This is probably because most people are naïve and think that it is a case of advertising "franchises for sale" in a publication, on a website, or on a card in the corner shop and people will queue up to buy an area. It is such a good business, why-ever not?!

Part Two of this book explains the planning, the process, the procrastination, the pitfalls and the profits that all combine when you run a franchise business.

Where to start? Well, here is the thing: it really doesn't matter what business it is as long as it fits at least four if not all of the six points below;

1. A large market potential with regular repeat order potential
2. Products or a service with value for money
3. Easy to learn
4. Expandable to allow additional staff
5. Adaptable to technological changes over time
6. Generates good margin at mid-range pricing

This list may seem a little vague on first impressions, so let us look at each in turn to clarify the definition.

A large market potential with regular repeat order potential

The market potential really refers to the "served market". This is determined by research of a potential area or multiple areas, using demographics that provide an idea of all households or businesses that could use the product and then how many are likely to want to buy products or services, and how many may have already bought. For example if a defined area has 10,000 restaurants, pubs, nursing homes or indeed any businesses, then if the products could be used by everyone the market potential is of course 10,000. We all know that not everyone says yes and some prefer to shop at the cash-and-carry or supermarket for the products that you offer, so let us say half would buy and so the "served market" has dropped to 5,000. That means that there are 5,000 potential customers. If say 200–400 customers sustain a healthy business, then the market share required is 200–400 out of 5,000 or 4–8%, which is very good and shows a big market potential: one in twenty customers.

If this analysis shows that a franchisee must achieve a market share of 30% to have a profitable business then it will be more difficult, but not unachievable.

Repeat order potential is where the products or services are necessities that have to be bought every day, week or month. Luxuries are products or services that don't need to be bought and therefore are the first ones people stop ordering to save costs when times are tough.

Products or services offered at value

To generate a profitable business, you must understand your business and the products or services that are offered, ensuring that they are provided at competitive prices for the area that they are sold into. Pricing is even more important in franchising because the franchisee needs turnover and margin to generate a gross profit out of which he pays the franchisor a royalty, pays operating costs and then takes drawings to make a living.

If you currently sell an item for £2 and it costs £1 to make, or buy and sell, then your business makes a pound profit for every item sold. If a franchisee sells the same item for £2 and he buys it from you for £1, you lose the £1 profit, unless you now enjoy economies of scale and lower distribution costs because you use franchisees and buy more.

This example is fine for the UK, however in the US legislation makes it difficult to sell products direct to franchisees, although some franchisors stateside do sell direct. However, it is often simpler to outsource third party suppliers and avoid the legislative constraints.

If the products or services rendered are excellent, then comparison can actually deliver sales growth by highlighting a real benefit that adds value. For example, dilution or durability has a value if explained properly to a potential customer. For many years Fairy Liquid used this approach and stated in their advertisements that every bottle washed many more dishes compared to another leading brand. We then saw a pile of crockery that showed the gawping viewer real value, even if it was a few pence more. Durability is another way of explaining value, if quality materials are used and the product lasts five years compared to the three-year average life of a product from a competitor who uses inferior materials. If the cost of the superior product is 20% more, the customer will save money.

Easy to learn

A simple transfer of information to a potential franchisee so that they don't spend months learning and not earning is crucial. Something that can be taught in a few weeks and then put into practice will be more successful than something that needs supervision almost every day for a long period of time.

If it could take months, then franchising your business will be difficult and perhaps employing people and training them as specialists might be a better option.

Expandable to allow additional staff

This refers to future potential so that the opportunity to employ more people to maximise the potential is a definite option. Whether a franchisee will expand is an entirely different decision for them later, but showing them the opportunity to dramatically increase turnover with a relatively small increase in market share increases the perceived potential. The bigger the market is then the more opportunity there is to expand. A great example of an expandable offering is a coffee bar or fast food outlet. If the first location delivers profit, then a second in an equally good location will offer potential to build a mini-empire.

Adaptable to technological changes over time

Of course we cannot see into the future, but if the product or service offered is based on older technology then upgrading and staying at the cutting edge is crucial or the whole business may disappear. This includes product development to ensure better results and continued value for money.

Generates good margin at mid-range pricing

I have already hinted at this but further clarification is important to reinforce the need for good pricing that isn't either the cheapest or the most expensive. The pricing should deliver a margin to allow a potential franchisee to generate individual profit and benefit from being in business at all. Ideally, if a franchisee can buy from you at £1 and sell to the end user for £1.80 to £2.20, then they will be able to sell enough to pay for stock and overheads and pay themselves. This is often a difficult concept to understand for businesses looking to franchise as they see an erosion of profits by having to sell wholesale to franchisees instead of having the luxury of selling at full price. What has to be established is the wholesale price that still provides a small margin for the franchisor and covers distribution cost whilst the erosion is off-set by the royalty or licence fee that will be received. I will address this in detail later in the book.

Perhaps I am being a little harsh in suggesting that all six points need to be achieved, but four or five at the very least must be achievable or adaptable, otherwise any venture into franchising will fail.

Make sure that you understand the potential market and how easy it is to transfer information to franchisees in the future so that they can build a business and make profits without daily support from you; otherwise expanding with employees is your best option.

This could work – Creating a new concept to franchise

Every day people have wonderful ideas. They jump-start their brain on the way to work or at home, trying to think about something that is unique and the proverbial pot of gold at the end of the rainbow.

Entrepreneurs gain our admiration and respect when they bring an idea to the masses and create demand that generates sales. How often have we said "why didn't I think of that?" to friends and family. Quite right as well. Something simple, something nobody has done before, can make us seek another unique or simple idea. Those blessed with the "idea of the decade" then often want to roll out the business quickly and capitalise on the potential before someone else copies the idea. This is where franchising can be the answer.

The problem with franchising a new concept is a level of scepticism if the concept has not yet been proven. For the originator the risk is divulging a new concept to the world and therefore potentially letting others copy the idea, especially if the concept is not protected by trademark or copyright.

This is somewhat of a quandary for the genius who dreamt up the new and exciting concept, however good ideas have made some of the greatest concepts in the world of franchising today.

The idea, perhaps your idea reading this, may be a variation on a common theme, a different way of bringing something to the market. Coffee bars are a great example – delivering a different way of grabbing a cup of the brown liquid and getting away with charging £3.00 for something that may previously have cost £1.00 at a café. The variation is dynamic, a variety of frothy styles that can have sprinkles, in a cardboard cup. Superlattemocca made with soya milk is a far cry from the "Cona" filter in a crockery cup, but essentially coffee nonetheless.

Making the coffee bar part of the High Street or shopping mall has taken time and with Starbucks, Costa and copycat operations franchised in almost every country, the growth of the "coffee bar" concept has been phenomenal to say the least.

Great concepts commonly work well in franchising if the provision of product or a service appears affordable and lets the buyer, be that a business or homeowner, gain time to do something else instead or avoid a mundane and despised task. An example of this is oven cleaning; it is messy and rarely leaves the oven gleaming. Getting someone to use aggressive products is worth the money for many, especially when the time could be better spent elsewhere.

It is very easy to get excited about a wacky idea that would make a great franchise concept – the difficulty is getting people to buy into your enthusiasm if it is unique and unproven.

I didn't realise that – Some of the downsides

You can't decide one day to franchise a business and launch it the next.

To get it right takes time and investment and unless the founder has knowledge of franchising there is a definite need for external help from a specialist or expert to make sure mistakes are not made that can bring down the whole business.

Downsides are only risks, and as long as people are aware of them they are merely obstacles that can be avoided or navigated around.

The biggest risk is the potential to lose control of a method or system by introducing franchisees to the brand. This is a risk that is apparent for any franchise, even the established ones. It is a risk that you have to take, but good controls and a comprehensive agreement will protect your business.

Come in Traffic Control

Perhaps the need to provide a pilot scheme is the biggest surprise, especially when someone is keen to franchise and roll a concept out quickly. A pilot scheme is so important because it will show that an individual has built a business quickly and generated an income. This is the biggest selling point when a franchise launches but it takes time; six months, maybe even a year. It is worth remembering that banks will lend up to 70% of the cost to future franchisees, but only if a pilot scheme has run for 12 months minimum to take account of seasonal fluctuations. This may seem an unnecessary delay for the impatient entrepreneur, a downside. You can bypass the pilot scheme with a proven company-run system but analysis of a territory cost centre also takes time to create. There is more detailed information on pilot schemes in Chapter Ten but it is important to mention the need for a form of pilot scheme in this section, when you are thinking about franchising.

Nugget... in a Nutshell

Pilot schemes not only prove the franchisable concept but help you sell the concept; this is why they are so important.

How much does it cost? – Financing the project

As with any business venture there is a risk, which normally equates to the potential financial loss if all goes wrong.

Franchising a business is no different; however the downside for many is the need to invest in a franchise agreement, which will cost at least £5,000, linked to the use of a franchise consultant and the development cost of literature, a recruitment campaign and additional support staff at further cost. If you are really serious about franchising then you need to allocate at least £20-30,000 without any guarantee of any return.

This isn't the same for every country and so the best advice is to contact the franchise association in your country for advice on costs.

Accept that this investment is effectively research into a new market that is similar to companies investing in research and development of a product. The investment is needed to yield a return on investment over many years.

A piecemeal approach with staged investment is by far the best way to proceed so that you can invest in a basic overview report and then sign off further investment when detailed research and a strategic plan have been approved by stakeholders. By way of an example, let me break this down, exactly the same way that I would with a client. This is not a definitive guide and many consultants have their own approach that may differ from the following example. Yes, that is a disclaimer on my part!

Consultants and Costs

You really need external help to evaluate the franchise route. More importantly, you need unbiased appraisal without an ulterior motive to sell more consultancy services irrespective of whether the concept is good or bad.

I usually offer a free consultation to get an idea of the business and the owner's expectations. If I feel that it is a viable concept and I should dig a little deeper, then the next stage and first cost is to create an overview report.

This is spending one or two days working in the business, meeting staff, not just the principal, to gauge their suitability to a franchised concept; don't forget, they will be the support team of the future. After getting a better understanding of the market, the next step is pulling everything together in a brief report, with project timeline and future costs outlined so that the stakeholders can consider their options. The cost of this report depends on how much detail is required but I would charge anything from £2,000 upwards.

For most clients the overview report provides a snapshot of where to go and what is needed to prepare and launch their business. If the project appears too risky with some £2,000 spent then there is no further cost.

A more complex "Strategic Plan" for blue chip clients can take far longer, anything from two weeks to six months to research and prepare. For most new-start franchises two to three weeks is normally sufficient to compile a strategic plan.

A strategic plan is, by definition, a seven-step plan that covers key sections including financial models for two to five years and the possible exit and sale of the business, thus satisfying investors. A full strategic plan can cost anything from £5,000 to £25,000.

Plan Accepted – Next?

With the stakeholders' consent to proceed and positive about the opportunity to realise their dream of franchising their business, the next stage is to involve the management team in the business in the planning process. A consultant is far more cost effective than employing someone full time. Commissioning a consultant to create a detailed project that delivers pilot scheme evaluation, branding of the concept, marketing of the launch, staff training, franchisee training and the writing of the operation manual is the next cost, and £3,000 to £5,000 is a reasonable expectation.

Non-Executive Mentoring

Mentoring is another popular term in "business jargon". Effectively, it provides non-executive support for a day or two a month to ensure the project is running on time. It is important for a consultant to mentor, *not* dictate, and work with the stakeholders to offer an opinion on methods and ideas. People don't like change and the consultant should nurture staff effectively, selling the plan and their importance in the success of the plan.

As I have already suggested, every consultant works differently. However, for this example I would expect to secure commitment in the form of a monthly non-executive fee to mentor the project and ensure staff members complete their assigned tasks. The fees and days required to achieve the goal vary, depending on the timeline. A daily fee of £750–£1,000 is normal, although some consultants charge more. I normally offer a package linked to a non-executive role with ongoing access when not on site, as well as the contracted days, which means that for say £2,500 per month I will offer set days for board meetings and project review meetings with employees. Overall, this equates to £15,000 for six months. Compared to a full-time franchise director at say £60,000 a year, this is value for the client, in my opinion.

And Finally

The other costs are the associated artwork charges for literature and advertisements. With printing this will amount to some £4,000. The wording is part of the consultant's role in the process.

The franchise agreement will cost around £5,000 for a basic cut-and-paste version from a franchise solicitor and variations and specific conditions may add another £5,000, although a definitive all-in cost can be obtained at the beginning.

Let us total up the costs up to the point of advertising, six months into a project and with literature, agreement and advertorial pieces ready to go with the help of the consultant. For the £30,000 you will have spent you will have a professional model that can compete in the industry and attract new franchisees.

If you wish to do some of the work yourself then this cost can be reduced considerably, but why would you wish to divert attention from running your successful business? I always tell clients that their time is valuable and it will take them far longer to create something in franchise terms at what many

Don't try to set up a franchise alone, use a consultant as a far more economical route. Prepare to invest at least £30,000 to research the viability of your business as a franchise.

refer to as the opportunity cost of not doing something important to their business.

This is a brief overview of the costs, with more detail and expansion on the key areas later in the book.

10

Who's my Guinea Pig?

Testing the Concept

Flaps … Check, flight plan … Check … Pilot ready for take off!

Let's try it first – Setting up a pilot scheme

I mentioned the importance of a pilot scheme in the last chapter and without repeating much of what you may have just read, the rest of this chapter is more a detailed guide to overseeing a pilot scheme.

Pilot schemes are encouraged by the British Franchise Association, The International Franchise Association and other country or territory specific bodies, all of which are the organisations that oversee the development of franchising in an ethical manner. Membership of a franchise association isn't a definitive requirement to operate as a franchise but it does give credibility to those claiming compliance with ethical standards.

Principal Operated Pilot Schemes

In some cases the pilot scheme is the recorded information of the business owner, working alone from the start with no customers and then following a system. The sales and costs show the potential. This is incredibly basic but is often the example that franchisors use. The danger is that the system portrayed may be completely different for a franchisee; the cost of stock is different and commitments to leases may not be exactly the same. Massaging the figures will no doubt provide an example but in this litigious world, evidence may need to be provided in the future.

Employee Case Study Pilot Schemes

Using information gathered from employee sales records is often used as a pilot scheme example, although this is fraught with danger and open to dispute. It can be challenged later in court if it is used as a franchisee example. The employee has a guaranteed income and does not have the same pressure as a franchisee would, but the main pressure is still to "sell to earn". This type of pilot is a manufactured scheme and is often frowned upon by the industry as a quick fix to the problem of launching quickly.

Deciding not to have a pilot study at all and thus going to market without an example may be a better option, rather than turning into a fiction writer and creating a spurious example of a possible pilot. Although selling to potential franchisees with a proven pilot scheme will certainly help them in the decision-making process, it is not essential.

Test Pilots

One way of securing a pilot scheme without delaying the launch is to attract a small number of pilot franchisees, at a reduced initial fee. Recruiting, training and supporting two or three pilot franchisees for say six months, at which time information is available, is an excellent way of proving the system and maximising the chances of success. The incentive for pilot franchisees is less financial risk coupled with exceptional support because the franchisor is desperate for them to prove the system and succeed.

Once this type of pilot scheme is complete the test pilots can also assist in selling the concept to full-fee franchisees at the time of launch.

Convincing an employee to convert to a franchisee is a variation on this method and has the additional benefits of awareness of the company and systems; however data can be used to develop a pilot scheme. In some cases the sweetener for the employee is a free territory and even some financial support for a set period until the pilot scheme has been completed. There may also be a guarantee of their job back if they wish. The value of the pilot scheme to potential franchisors is that evaluation of the results enables them to tailor the launch.

There are lots of ways to carry out a pilot scheme and often it depends on how quickly you need to get to market. If a year-long pilot scheme may seriously impact on a market potential then consider an alternative way of presenting the concept to potential franchisees.

It works! – Analysing the success and understanding the market

Success is measured against achievable targets, and thereafter surpassing those targets.

Getting useful information from a pilot study is essential so that the features and benefits are clear when you are selling the concept to potential franchisees later.

Potential franchisees measure success by the monetary return compared to employment options. This has nothing to do with the number of customers or the margin achieved; if the profit is inadequate then they are not interested. People often refer to success as a "numbers game", which is a simple way of saying, for example, approach 100 people, see 50, gain interest from 25 and finally sell to 15. If the 15 have value then fine, and if you require 150 to make the business profitable then by definition you must approach 1000.

Franchisees eventually need to make a profit, and figures on a spreadsheet mean very little on their own. I often consider the example of what a pilot franchisee has achieved as the most important information. This includes the number of sales calls, appointments gained and the conversion rate. This tells me what they are doing and how well they are doing it. If the conversion is low then perhaps additional sales training is required as part of the franchise model. This may include additional field support.

Stay in Contact!

Keeping track of weekly figures and speaking to the pilot franchisees at least once a week also allows you to live the experience with them and consider small changes that may benefit the scheme and future franchisees whilst recording data in a logical manner to allow you to develop a profit example based on fact, not fiction.

Number Crunching

Measuring success against a predefined target must include an understanding of monthly costs and expected losses as the pilot area is developed. Any business expects to lose money in the initial set-up stages and the key factor in evaluating the overall data captured is the time to reach break-even and thereafter profit. This is what a potential franchisee will consider before signing up.

Franchisors are often worried about telling potential franchisees that they will lose money until they are established, but why? It is surely better to warn someone that they are not buying a job and that they need money to support the growth of their business for the first few months and then to cover the household bills until cash and profit are achieved.

Showing a real profit example, created from actual data, adds weight to the discussion and shows candour, which in turn builds trust between a potential franchisee and the franchisor.

Even if the sales and profit figures are lower than expected there may be lessons learned from analysing the market. There might be a requirement to alter wholesale or retail prices to accommodate a need to generate higher sales or margin to make the concept more attractive. This is far easier to achieve in the pilot stage.

In some cases a price increase may generate more profit for less work at prices acceptable in the market. Many business gurus consider a price increase a far better strategy than price cuts and working harder for the same profit. Again, the implementation of such a strategy is far easier during the pilot scheme stage.

Reviewing Personal Strengths and Weaknesses

The final part of any analysis concerns the individual or collective pilot scheme participants. Much the same as employers review their employees' strengths and weaknesses, franchisors must analyse pilot franchisees. Data is fine but if the figures are exceptional because a pilot franchisee is a wonderful salesperson then presenting this as the definitive guide in the future is a false representation of the average candidate. Alternatively, if the pilot franchisee is a poor salesperson the figures may be low.

Business analysis is based on judgement and consideration of all external factors before deciding on average performance, realistic targets and thereafter a measure of success.

Try to remember that people have different backgrounds and skills and in franchising a new approach is required to recruitment. There is a huge difference between having the luxury to employ the best people in a company and recruiting franchisees, which initially at least is about attracting candidates and accepting average people with good potential, and enough motivation and tenacity to succeed. If you ask 100 franchisors whether they would employ every franchisee in their network and any one of them said yes then they would be lying, a huge lie, and a lie to end all lies!

The fact remains that you may wish to attract the best but you cannot achieve growth if you do not accept less than the best.

Successful "over-achievers" making very good money from running their business within a franchise system normally represent 20% of the total number and these will provide you with 80% of your profit. The remainder will generate 20% of profits and take up 80% of your time. This may sound crazy but remember that out of your whole network approximately 30% are making a living and are hopefully satisfied with their business, while 30% are growing and 20% under-achieve. Perhaps these are new franchisees or those not suited to self-employment at all. Collectively this 80% needs more support, which you hope will increase their turnover and profits until they graduate into the top 20% bracket and thus require less support.

When analysing a pilot scheme try to imagine different types of people from different walks of life and how easy it will be for them to pick up the tricks of the trade.

Land grab – How large should an area be?

One of the offshoots of a pilot scheme is the informed consideration of how effective an operative is in a given area. Territory planning may be an effective way of managing time but in my experience franchisees often travel too far to get an order and spend an inordinate amount of time and money on fuel to service a customer far, far away. The reason is simple; people initially scour their area to find customers and often drive to the extreme because it is easier to drive than sell. When they do target a potential customer on the border of their area they work harder to get that customer because in some way it shores up the border and protects their business. Another reason is that their products or services are more acceptable in the countryside, with less competition from other businesses located in cities or towns.

It is wise to consider the information obtained from the pilot scheme to help you decide a suitable area size.

Historically, the biggest mistake territory-based franchisors make is granting large areas to new franchisees and they often rue the day when they have nothing left to sell. When they look at the turnover in each area it is abundantly clear that although sales are evident they have many franchisees who could grow more business but do not wish to invest in employees or additional locations. This is a sticking point in a two-sided agreement, all due to the fact that they have sold an area far too large for a sole trader franchise to be effective.

Hands up, I have been guilty of this error as well, especially with newer franchises because it is a way of securing a franchisee when it is imperative to show to other potential franchisees that the concept is attractive and other people have signed up.

Don't Sell Massive Areas!

This is where effective and strong management of the territories is important before launch. The best way to do this is to analyse the information gained from a pilot scheme. By plotting the spread of customers in the pilot territory relative to the turnover and cost of going to those customers, it becomes clear what effect reducing an area would have. You should aim for busy franchisees in a smaller area linked to the potential customers in the area so that the "numbers game" philosophy still works.

Plot the Map

A good way of planning a network and multiple areas is to get a large postcode map, with sub-postcodes, from a supplier such as Map Marketing. It may be better to get a number of maps that, when placed together, cover a wall and show the whole country eight feet tall. If you plan to have a network of say 100 eventually, then creating say 150 areas is prudent because it is unlikely that a vast area such as the Scottish Highlands will sell quickly, if at all, especially if the concept is suited to larger concentrations of households or small businesses.

Sub-dividing a city into two, three or four areas also depends on the concept, however it is a good idea to do this anyway so that, for example, Birmingham has four territories, each with an acceptable number of chimney pots. Thus one area may include postcodes B15–B64.

Digital mapping software is also available with a variety of options so that you may define areas and print maps quickly in the future.

This approach has two advantages. It provides a perception of the network eventually, when an even spread of franchisees has been achieved. It also allows the option of selling additional areas to franchisees if they wish to invest in larger management-driven areas by acquiring a larger territory coupled with investment in infrastructure.

Revisiting Areas

Even though your territories are defined I guarantee that you will revisit territories when you start to recruit new franchisees. The reason is simple; again, potential franchisees always want a huge area similar to the gold prospectors in California in the Nineteenth Century. This is why, when faced with a deal breaker, you will concede at least one negotiation because you have to secure franchisees. Don't despair though, there are clever ways to combine the need to secure franchisees and maintain a strong control. Grant a number of larger areas to the first influx of franchisees with a target clause agreed so that if a target growth is not achieved then you, as franchisor, have the right to take back some of the area if another potential franchisee wants to buy. Write a suitable but minimal compensation for handing over customers into the agreement, or as an attachment in the schedule. Alternatively, allowing a franchisee to trade in adjoining areas until that area is sold may placate a franchisee.

Many franchisors prefer territory-based franchises but an increasing number of free-range concepts are evident today. Although the problems associated with poaching and transfer of customers evaporates, there can be problems with saturation of a town or city with competing franchisees from the same business. Many concepts have flourished without territory constraints in the last twenty years: concepts such as Chips Away International with over 300 UK franchises and in some cases five or six in a city, all turning over good figures.

Subway is another example of massive growth without territory constraints. Subway franchisees open a location and then, if another potential franchisee shows interest, they have the option to open another location or not in a given timeframe. As I understand it from knowing some of the US franchisees, if they decide not to then the location is sold and another Subway store may appear at the other end of a street, a few blocks away. This approach has certainly contributed to the massive growth of Subway in the UK and replicates the US success story, with Subway visible in almost every shopping mall and strip mall.

Whether your concept is launched with defined territories or not is a decision that depends on the growth plan and the level of security or protection that you wish to sell to potential franchisees. If you do decide on a territory-based concept then you must be prepared to answer potential franchisees if they want evidence that the given area is large enough for them to succeed. It is very important to ensure careful planning, and to have the belief that the areas created can sustain a business before launching the concept at franchise exhibitions or in the press.

11

Is This a Goldmine?

Working Through the financials

This is great – time for a bigger safe!!!

Jigsaw in front of me – Now put it together

Financial models are like a big jigsaw; you have to find the pieces and then put them into the right places so that the picture is complete when the last piece is fitted into the last gap.

Most people use spreadsheet programmes, such as Microsoft Excel, as the business format to create financial budgets. Some financiers use bespoke software programme to plan and budget income and expenditure.

If you have used complex software before then this section is fairly easy. If you are not confident in creating spreadsheets then seek a little advice from a consultant or your accountant.

It is important to find the pieces of the jigsaw, and there are plenty to find, so that when your financial model is complete the picture is as accurate as you can make it, based on the assumptions made.

A good spreadsheet document lets you change a figure or assumption and the auto-calculation uses the formula to save you rehashing the front sheet every time.

Each of the sub-sections in this chapter will provide you with a way to get the values for your venture. After that, the spreadsheet savvy person excels at inserting the information into a relevant back-sheet or the front page, if you excuse the pun!

Checklist – What should my spreadsheet include?

What indeed. This depends on how deep you want to go and how much justification you wish to have for your figures.

There are a number of categories that I think you should consider and, more importantly for franchising, the income streams are all driven by a sales matrix. It is a table in very plain English that has the number of recruited franchisees and the running total of franchisees operating, by month. An example is below.

	A	B	C	D	E	F	G	H	I	J	K	L	M
1	Month	1	2	3	4	5	6	7	8	9	10	11	12
2	New	0	1	1	1	2	2	2	2	2	2	2	3
3	Existing	0	0	1	2	3	5	7	9	11	13	15	17
4	Total	0	0	2	3	5	7	9	11	13	15	17	20

With a sales matrix you can use the grid reference and the value in a formula from another sheet, for example box E4 = 3, and so elsewhere in the spreadsheet if you have say £500 licence fees for each franchise, then multiplying the value by E4 auto-calculates £1500. If you change any values then the matrix multiples auto-calculate any reference to the number of franchisees. Don't forget to create a formula for the totals though in the matrix!

The following list is only a guide and not exhaustive by any means.

- Income – Franchisors enjoy multiple income streams including:
  ○ Franchise Fees
  ○ Licence Fees (Royalties)
  ○ Product or Service Supply Sales (Wholesale)

- Expenditure – The usual so-called fixed costs are easy to enter into a spreadsheet although some assumptions are required:
  ○ Rent

- ○ Rates
- ○ Salaries
- ○ Telephones
- ○ Travel
- ○ Insurances
- ○ Advertising
- ○ Stationery
- ○ Miscellaneous Costs

- Variable Franchise Costs – the following list is driven by the sales matrix because the associated cost is applied if you have new franchisees in a particular month or the number operating drives an income stream:
  - ○ Set-up Costs – uniforms, insurances, training etc.
  - ○ Stock Costs – ongoing supplies and initial stock for franchisees joining
  - ○ Additional travel

It is very easy to over-complicate financial models but the best ones take into account the impact of potential recruitment and the growth of the franchise income with the obvious need to finance support in the early stages.

Nugget... in a Nutshell

Financial models can be as detailed as you like, but you have to remember that although you believe in the concept this doesn't simply translate to incredible recruitment figures. Be conservative when setting income values and over-estimate costs to make sure that you don't rely purely on new franchisees to break even. Ensure you have capital available to finance the venture in the fledgling years.

Financial models become easier in future years with concrete information and informed assumptions; however for this chapter the luxury of this historic information is not available. This is where research and best guesstimates are your only option.

It will cost you this – Deciding on a true franchise fee

What is a fair franchise fee? A fee that someone wants to pay is the easy answer. So that's it, a quick simple chapter, or maybe not.

Setting the right price needs a little thought and even the help of a franchise consultant. If the price is too low you may attract the wrong people whilst adding cost instead of profit to your business. Set the price too high and you may not recruit anyone.

That helps, I hear you say! Sorry, I sound guarded, as if I am avoiding an answer at all costs; however the fact remains that a scientific approach to this quandary works if all factors are considered.

You can, of course, use industry averages. For example, the average initial fee is £15,000–£20,000, with average licence fees of 8%. Using averages can be misleading though as they are exactly that – industry averages. It is far better to take into account similar franchises and, more importantly, work out the true franchise fee and licence fee values from the ground up.

There is a real possibility of over-complicating this chapter, so I will attempt to keep the rationale concise.

What a Franchise Fee Includes

The franchise fee should cover a small honorarium for the territory and the remainder should cover the training and ongoing support.

Adopting this ethical approach allows you to build a real fee from the ground upwards, whilst justifying the charges. First add up the tangible items that you provide, such as stock at the wholesale price that you would charge a franchisee to buy from you, stationery, store fittings, computers, uniforms and marketing costs. This is a definitive figure that is easy to explain and justify.

Second is the training cost, including the time at the head office or facility with any accommodation, food and direct costs such as room hire. Adding the staff cost to run the course is another cigarette packet calculation, for example if the course is two weeks long and the training manager is paid £30,000 a year, a quick calculation assuming two weeks of their pay is $\frac{1}{26}$th of the salary, or £1,153.84, rounding this up to £1,500 covers employer's contributions and expenses.

The total of everything above is the set-up and initial training cost.

Future Cost of Support

Working out future cost requires the other side of the cigarette packet, I am afraid. The training manager will spend a day a week for the first six months and a day every other week for the rest of the year. Using the fag packet that is approximately another 35 days, from above, 1/52 of the annual salary with a bit of change to cover contributions and expenses equates to £750 a week, so seven weeks is approximated at £5,250 to provide support for one franchisee. If the number of days is less or more the same nicotine calculation applies.

While this is not entirely accurate as the employed support team includes administration and part involvement from more than one individual, it is a cost you can justify if you're questioned later and one that also clarifies the ongoing cost to you of support in the field.

This cost exercise will at the very least show you what you will pay out, the bare minimum to cover the set-up and training of a franchisee in the first year. Adding on the aforementioned honorarium for the piece of land attached to the overall fee is the tricky bit. A little is acceptable for most but doubling or trebling a ball-park figure is much like selling a house in Tibet at Mayfair prices. Nothing against Tibet here by the way, just in case a potential client from that wonderful country reads this, of course.

Let us assume that the total costs calculated are £17,500 and the territory fee of £5,000 is added. In my opinion this works and is totally justifiable later if you're questioned. In percentage terms it is a 30% fee for the right to trade and enjoy the benefits of being part of a bigger business.

With a rough idea of the possible fee, comparing it to similar franchise concepts is a good idea, a very good idea. Even if your idea is unique, comparing the basic style to a similar white collar, mobile or retail outlet will put your offering in a similar category if someone compares a wide range of franchises whilst researching franchising as an option.

Launch price is often different from the eventual price, with a lower price used to entice the first few franchisees so that training costs are covered. There is nothing wrong with setting an offer price for a short period and then using the success from your first influx to sell at a higher price, closer to the original fee calculated.

This figure, lower or higher, is the first line of your sales matrix that eventually feeds into the income for your little goldmine. Every franchisee recruited will generate a fee with a set-up cost incurred. Simple!

Working out a franchise fee requires a little science mixed with a pinch of assumption. The important note here is whatever the figure you calculate you must compare it to other similar styled franchises, as they are your main competition.

How many? – Annual recruitment potential

Working out the numbers expected is often pure speculation for a new franchise concept and in addition your euphoria and belief in the opportunity, as franchisor, clouds your evaluation of the potential recruitment levels. Why wouldn't everyone snap your hand off to get a piece of the action?

You need to temper your obvious belief in your system to ensure that you do not over-estimate targets for franchise recruitment. In addition to this, although you have not even interviewed a franchisee yet, it is wise to remember and use any experience you have in setting targets.

Every salesperson has come away from a meeting sure that they have secured a sale. After a great meeting with the buyer agreeing with every feature and benefit, the order is a mere formality. In reality, time kills sale and little voices on the buyer's shoulder start to get the better of the decision, resulting in a resounding "no" when "yes" was expected.

This is why sales managers and directors press salespeople to secure the order quickly, much to the anguish of the salesperson who would rather leave the customer to call them, after such a good presentation. With time killing orders, managers are sceptical of potential new business presented at sales meetings and ask what the percentage chance of securing an order are, and when the first order is expected. The salesperson will start with 100% chance, next week, but in most cases this will reduce after waiting a month or two for a decision to 25% in two months. This isn't a definitive analysis; although I am sure someone else has carried out research and worked out a time-line of the fallout rate.

It is no different when selling a franchise to someone. Buying signals may be there and the person in front of you may seem very keen to sign and start, but with all life-changing decisions the demons get to work and people subconsciously look for a reason not to make a decision. Thereafter, time kills the sale for the franchisor.

The difficulty for the franchisor is balancing the desire to sign a suitable candidate with the need to avoid a hard sell approach. No different from any sale.

It is easy to pluck a figure out of the air, and it may be as accurate as anything else that you do to estimate the possible recruitment.

A good way to set a realistic target is to see what other similar type concepts achieve, and researching into network strengths after a year is fairly easy. Information available on web portals for different companies, the franchise press and even the bfa show similar style franchises and those in the same price range. If say ABC franchise has recruited eight franchisees in the first year and ten in the second year, whilst DEF franchise has recruited six in the first year and twelve in the second year, then it is fair to assume similar figures as a bare minimum.

With an idea, again speculative but based on some analysis, entering the numbers of recruits into the sales matrix allows you to ascertain the income achieved and the relative costs and include them in your financial model. This is where a matrix allows you to move the number of recruits around to see the impact on cash and cost.

Set Values – What a Great Tool!

If the sales revenue is linked by formula to the profit and loss you will save time by avoiding the need to recalculate individual figures. For example if you change a recruit from month four (cell F66) to month six (cell H66) in the matrix all you have to do is change it on the matrix and the profit and loss will recalculate the income in month six in the profit and loss sheet (say cell H9) from a formula entered in that cell, such as = (H66)*(franchise fee) with the franchise fee set in the spreadsheet as £21,000. Or the formula could be = (H66)*21000. Microsoft Excel has a great help tutorial if you need help in this excellent tool for any business.

You can set formulae for set-up costs and all of the other variable franchise costs as well so that they auto-calculate in the cost side of the financial projections when the matrix is changed.

When setting franchise recruitment figures it is wise to phase the sales and allow for the initial launch period of at least three months before you sign a franchisee up. You could get very technical and budget the cash impact of fees received and set-up costs paid out but at the early stage it is perhaps better to account in the same month to make it easier to understand.

I am fully aware that some items may not be bought for franchisees when they sign up as part of the set-up fees, for example promotional items with minimum order values or uniforms, and if there are any large costs then removing these from the set-up cost and including them as stock items might be prudent. Or am I going too deep?

The cost for a training manager and other employees can be entered at the same time that you enter the recruitment estimates. A new administrator, needed when say four franchisees are recruited, can be entered as a cost in month X when the fourth franchisee is expected to start.

Playing with the matrix and seeing the impact of phased recruitment and even optimistic numbers is a good exercise in visualising the potential goldmine.

Estimating the recruitment level of new franchisees is not an exact science, so use information readily available of similar franchises already in the market.

Regular income – Licence fees and their importance

Licence fees or royalties are a contentious subject for franchisees, maybe not for the first year or so, but I can guarantee that the question of what they get for the monthly fee will come up as the franchisee matures and you develop your franchise business.

The licence income is a very important part of many franchise concepts globally. Many new franchisors use the licence fee "carrot" as another way of attracting franchisees, by reducing the ongoing charges to negligible or even fixed amounts. This is a good strategy as long as the other income streams are profitable. If they are not, the franchise is doomed.

Charging anything from 2%–20% of all franchise sales is usual, but your income is directly related to the success and turnover of the franchisees. Using a percentage system with phased growth by franchisee is the only way to accurately estimate licence fees. If you consider a fixed fee then the same calculation applies, with say £250 per month starting whenever the franchisee finishes training.

Some franchise companies don't charge licence fees at all and rely on higher margin from supplied products. This is fine as long as the franchisee cannot buy the product elsewhere, perhaps at a lower price. The advent of the internet has opened the globe for business as a single territory, with business people able to search for suppliers far more easily than before the magic of cyberspace. I am not saying that all franchisees seek lower supply prices, as most accept the benefit of being part of a network which often means best prices collectively; however there is always someone looking to move stock at a lower margin. In my opinion the best franchise concepts have a balance of three income streams with products, licence fees and franchise sales. Therefore even if you wish to keep licence fees to a minimum you have to consider the product turnover and small margin derived from each franchise area sold.

In truth, all income streams are incredibly important to your overall income and cash flow and as far as the financial model is concerned it is prudent to consider a contingency of say 10% for late licence fees at the end of the first year just in case some franchisees fall a little behind in payments.

How you set up the licence fee calculation is also important. If your concept relies on franchisees making prompt weekly sales declarations, backed up by copy invoices let's say, then the oldest trick in the book is to delay making the returns so that the invoice for licence fees is also delayed. This is why so many franchisors have decided to levy a set fee which in turn reduces the administration factor for calculating licence fees. A strong regime or, even better, one that records sales electronically via point-of-sale software, precludes the use of this trick.

Watch out – Watch out, There's a Dodger About!

This is probably the right time to explain some other tricks that franchisees use to avoid paying licence fees. This may appear underhand and not congruent with the positive tones of this guide, however franchisees use tricks, no matter how unpalatable they appear at the planning stage. Being made aware of such tricks is to be forewarned, which is important when you consider the heavy investment needed to launch a concept.

Which Books are the Real Ones?

Yes, sometimes two sets of books are created, especially if the sales reporting is based on manual copies. For some reason franchisees think that submitting some invoices will placate the franchisor, who will not investigate further. The warning signs are low sales and a franchisee apparently happy and not crying for help. Comparing stock purchased to sales made and reported will also enable you to calculate an individual margin and if this is lower than the average there might be some skulduggery. Another way to uncover fraud is to check VAT returns against sales declared. Deceiving the franchisor is one thing but the government is a whole different ball game!

Rollercoaster Reporting

Some franchisors offer capped licence fees with benefit to the franchisees who hit a certain level of sales. The licence fee payable is a maximum amount, and sales above the set figure are free of licence fee!

If a cap system is used then the franchisees can benefit from their success. However, the system must be solid, with qualifying criteria of achieving the target for say three months. Thereafter the franchisee agrees to join the scheme and is charged the cap fee whether or not the target sales are achieved.

If the cap system is variable then franchisees will exploit this, no question, and report a high figure one month, pay a capped licence fee, then report a low figure at the actual percentage charged, alternating a bumper sales month with a poor month to reduce their fees.

The introduction of a capped licence fee is a fabulous selling tool when you're talking to potential franchisees and as long as the capped fee is factored into the financial model it also provides you as the franchisor with a more accurate income stream evaluation. Of course the capped fees will normally only kick in after some time, when franchisees have developed their business to a fairly high turnover.

Other Income Fees – Advertising or Marketing Levies

Some franchisors also charge a separate advertising levy, fixed or variable, with the fund used to promote the brand for the benefit of everyone. This is another income stream but in reality the funds received are all used to advertise the products or services. Problems start when franchisors use the fund to promote franchise recruitment, using the excuse that having more franchisees benefits incumbent operators by improving the buying power and brand awareness. This is dangerous and is probably why many franchisors use a management franchisee group that meets to agree promotion beneficial to franchisees as well as the brand. These groups usually include two or three franchisees elected by the network, with two or three company people to maintain the balance. If there is an impasse on a particular strategy then often the franchisor will have the final say anyway, after considering the various opinions fully, thus retaining control of the brand.

One final point about licence fees and their importance is that ideally the licence fees cover the cost of the support function, allowing the income generated from franchise recruitment to further develop the network growth whilst the products or services sold generate the margin for the franchisor. This is the optimal mix, although in reality it is often not this simple.

Make sure that you understand the different licence fee options and their associated benefits and pitfalls, including the fee dodgers that can damage your venture.

Mix the information up and make some sense – Analysing the set-up cost and potential

There is much to consider at the pre-launch stage of any franchise. Perhaps the last two sections have opened up a can of worms, perhaps not, but it does show the importance of the income streams, how they impact on a profit and loss model and whether there is a goldmine or not, right in front of you.

Creating a sound spreadsheet model takes time initially but provides you with a great tool going forward. With formula driven sheets, small changes provide instant impact on profit and loss and this means that you can react quickly to strategic changes or recognise the impact of higher or lower recruitment figures.

Notwithstanding how important it is for a franchisor to believe in the potential of their concept, the positivity must be transferrable to potential franchisees and investors or financers. Because of this fundamental fact you have to work through the figures not once but at least three times to make sure that all the costs are included and that you have enough capital to support the plan, with a contingency plan as back-up if the recruitment is slower than anticipated.

Business is all about taking a risk, and franchising needs entrepreneurial spirit to grow as an industry. The creation of a financial model is a belt and braces approach and the advice offered will make you aware of things that you should consider.

When you have your jigsaw completed check that you didn't wedge a piece in the wrong place.

If you use formula-driven spreadsheets, check that the links work properly – then check again!

12

This is my Plan
Creating a Strategic Plan

Shall I use the road atlas as I go or the satellite navigation planned route? – How much detail is too much detail?

Where do I start? – Collating the research and financials and developing a strategic plan

Now, the author is a strategist so you totally expect a section on full strategic plans, correct?

Absolutely right but here is the reality check. Strategic plans are only useful if you stick to the plan, constantly refer to it and adapt the plan accordingly. The truth is that most plans, created with the best of intentions, sit in a filing drawer destined for a life under a directory. Management teams become too busy working in the business instead of working on the business. Why does this happen? Because being reactive is often easier that being proactive, the satisfaction of sorting one problem and then another problem fills the day at work. It is a comfort zone that most of us prefer, a safe place where no one can judge us by development criteria. The alternative zone is discomfort, with people judging valuable time in dreamland, innovating and mapping ways to get better.

Strategy is a word that people often associate with the military, chess or a computer game, not business planning. When I use the word I am careful that it does not give the impression of fancy business jargon.

Perhaps the biggest problem that people encounter is introducing change. People don't like change, especially if the same things have always worked for employees.

Why do we create plans? Most business managers don't plan in any detail but do plan at least one thing every day, even if it is what time to fit lunch in, make a call to someone, pick the children up or how to get from A to B in the quickest time. Perhaps all of these basic examples are not detailed planned business activities but reactionary functions, when the activity required fits into a gap in your day. Business orientated planning might be a board meeting, a review of the sales revenue or calls to potential customers.

Time management is a "plan for today" and is a great start if people want to develop creative time, no matter what they do for the rest of their day. Despite the urge to enter into pages of narrative on how time management is part of the skill set of a decent planner, I will simply refer to a great book, "How to Get Control of your Time and Your Life" by Alan Lakein, the godfather of time management. If you suffer from procrastination or never seem to have enough time in the day, week or month for everything you know that you should do, read this book. If you apply the philosophy you will create time for tasks and a greater freedom in your life.

You need to enjoy planning if you wish to create a strategy for the business, on paper at least; if you do not, then task an employee to do it or get advice from a consultant, which is your most cost-effective option.

What is a Strategic Plan?

Good strategic plans follow a step-by-step process and can include as much detail as you wish. I have written plans that have taken me weeks to research and weeks to write, with the whole process taking months. Others have taken a few days. The reason is that some require infinite detail and input from key personnel, with external data capture and definitive analysis and virtually no assumption.

Most plans do require a level of assumption and in franchising this is definitely the case. The key assumptions concern recruitment figures and thereafter the individual franchisee's performance. In the last chapter we looked at the science and guesstimates used to put a value on recruitment figures to create an overview of potential income and expenditure. Although this might appear out of kilter when you read the rest of this chapter, it makes sense if you want to analyse the potential before you invest in a full plan. The good thing is that the financial information created will slot into this detailed plan, so that work is already complete, save any adjustments after further research which flags a fundamental mistake.

A good plan has seven sections, a discussion of could which once more could take up reams of paper. That would be overkill in a general guide to franchising your business, therefore I resisted the temptation to spout too much information and have included only the salient points for you to consider.

Mission Statement

This is a statement of intent and is an excellent exercise to focus your mind on why you are in business and what you hope to achieve from franchising your business.

For some people this may seem somewhat dramatic. You may consider that you may have a very clear idea of what you hope to achieve, but does it translate to everyone else? Your conversations and memos might appear clear to you but to others they may be riddled with obfuscation! What? I hear you cry. Exactly. I used a word that isn't heard every day but when I explain that to "obfuscate" is to make something obscure or difficult to understand, the hidden message should be clear now: what someone hears or reads may not be how your speak or write.

Start by explaining in a single sentence what your business does. The second sentence should be what makes your business different from your competitors and finally what you would like the business to be in the future. Try to avoid portraying the business as the best thing since sliced bread if it isn't, although hoping it will be is perfectly acceptable.

For example:

"As a provider of innovative cost effective consultancy services to clients globally for many years, Franology intends to grow its portfolio of successful franchise operators and provide simple but effective ongoing advice for mutual benefit and gain."

Keep it simple and use common words when you write a mission statement.

Market

You may think that you already know the market but a full understanding is required so you need to find out the size of the market for the products or services that you offer, even if it is a new and unique concept.

As this is a fundamental question that potential franchisees will ask, it is not only important to the plan but important to state.

Ascertaining the market size is difficult if quantifiable information is not available. Larger companies have the luxury of using specific market research on a sample audience, but this might not be a viable option for your concept and budget.

The internet offers a wealth of information, especially government statistics and market research carried out by trade associations. This information may also have a breakdown, say of value by age group brackets, income levels, business turnover, and number of employees, or even by colour of the product!

Hopefully this information has a total market size or value, which you can further break down depending on specific criteria for your concept. For example, if your product is used by 18–30 year olds and you have figures available for different age groups, you can strip out those above and below from the total market. This smaller figure may be reduced further if you have information available on, say, male and female, or disposable income of over £10,000 per annum. Whatever the criteria, the reduced figure is the "served market" and your real market value available for your concept and thus potential franchisees.

If it is a new concept or a growing market the value might increase dramatically and you must consider this. A good example of this is mobile phones. Twenty years ago mobile phones were a luxury for many of us and now even seven year old kids have them. How big is that market and how much has it grown in two decades?

Likewise, if the market is saturated with technological improvements you must consider the constant investment into research and development and how this impacts on your plan.

For your research ask the question "How do you expect the market to change as you enter the arena, and why?" If you can quantify the answer rationally then it should be part of your plan and market research.

Competition

Businesses often forget to consider the competition and waft the potential impact on their "baby" away in a dismissive manner. This is usually because there is a lack of respect for another operator, most likely based on a brief but negative encounter. Either that or they cannot be bothered to find out who the major competitors are, and how good or bad they are.

Instead of dismissing a local or national chain of possible competitors, try researching and then analysing them as part of your plan. How much research you carry out depends entirely on the market you intend to compete in.

Nine times out of ten a business person will only look at the prices that a competitor charges and use this information as the impact factor on their business. This is very dangerous, in my view, as price is only a small part of a competitor's impact.

The first step is to consider the "served market". Then find out the major competitors and how much of that market they have. Check with Companies House, purchase filed accounts via the "Web Check" service and ascertain turnover as a percentage of the market. If the competitor operates in a number of markets, for example Tesco, which has the obvious food sales but also mobile phones, DVDs and pharmaceutical items, then it is a little more tricky. However, for most franchise concepts there are obvious major competitors that operate solely in your potential market.

If there are lots of little competitors, bunch them together as "others". A good example of this is portable appliance testing (PAT). There are a few bespoke companies with a few percent of the market share but over 85% of the market is serviced by small local electricians who test as an add-on service to their main activities.

You should then analyse the four or five main competitors and look at their strengths and weaknesses. Assuming what strategies they might have is also part of this research section in the overall plan.

An excellent evaluation method is to write the name of each major competitor on a sheet of paper and then list their strengths and weaknesses. Consider their image, products or services, customer service, financial stability and any information you can find on the management team, and then gauge whether they are ambitious, or happy to remain in a comfort zone.

Scan the trade press and find out whether there are any announcements about expansion or investment that may or may not point to any of their strategies.

After this exercise you will have a better idea of who your competitors are and what they are good or bad at. More importantly, you'll have a fair idea of what effect they could have on your business venture.

Self Evaluation and Consolidating the Environment

This is the business person's "honesty box", where they must look at the business and compare it to the same sections as above for the competitors.

This section of the plan considers the information from the previous section and thereafter you need to bring your findings together. This is called 'consolidating the environment'.

In basic terms, this is how you compare your strengths and weaknesses against those of your competitors, which will hopefully show both your opportunities and the threats to your business.

Businesses have carried out SWOT analyses (Strengths, Weaknesses, Opportunities and Threats) for years. They are not new but they are useless if they do not form part of the overall strategic plan and give due consideration to competitors. This part of the planning process looks at the controllable environment, your business, and the uncontrollable environment, your competitors. Combining the two by way of consolidating the whole environment brings everything together.

From all of the pieces of paper on each major competitor and your business, it should be clear where your opportunities are. For example, if a competitor has poor customer service levels, old technology or even a declining market share, there is an "opportunity" for you to capture their market share. On the other side of the coin, if a competitor has an expansion plan, a new fleet of vehicles, a new sales initiative, recently secured a national contract or has sole access to better technology, this is a "threat" to your venture and you must consider a way of bridging the gap.

I often refer to this part of the plan as the foundation for the real intention, which is to develop a set of objectives and strategies to achieve your targets and succeed in your objectives.

Objectives, Strategies, Programmes and Goals

Combined, these four words can instil fear into someone not used to writing a business plan. Break this section down into four categories and you will see that they are a good way of focusing the mind on your opportunities and how to achieve your target.

This section requires common sense rather than business acumen. For me, this is the exciting bit of a plan, with commitment to what you are going to do to succeed.

I have written this section more times than I care to admit, because it is so easy to over-complicate the process. The step process is more easily explained in the simple linked diagram below.

Opportunity ☐ Objective ☐ Strategy ☐ Programme ☐ Goal

Perhaps I can further explain this in a phrase or rule; maybe I should call this Gibson's Law –maybe not!

> "For every *Opportunity* or *Threat* a business encounters it must decide on an *Objective* to achieve the opportunity or combat the threat and agree on a proper *Strategy* whilst implementing a structured *Programme* of actions to achieve the desired *Goal*."

You present this in your plan either in bullet point format or in tabular format, depending on how much detail you want to go into.

If you want to show a diagram to simplify the plethora of words and information, then simply give each point in your table a number, e.g. Strategy 1, and then you can link any multiple points using lines, a little like the following diagram. This is called linkages and shows the reader a process map to your focused approach.

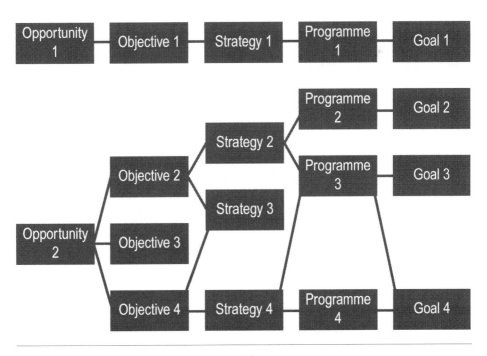

As you can see, one Programme may help you achieve one or more of your Goals and a Strategy may require a combination of Programmes.

Remember to include Threats as well, which may have the same Strategies to combat the risk to your business.

Resources

Any plan requires people to make it succeed. This might be one new employee or the use of a consultant or marketing specialist as part of the programmes highlighted in the previous section.

This is why the resource analysis fits into a strategic plan after due consideration to all of the previous sections, and not before, otherwise the plan would become unstable.

Resources are normally additional people or head count but also include investment in technology, premises and even the advertising budgets required. A few words of text to justify your assumptions are usually included under each potentially required resource. This shows the reader that you have investigated and considered the necessary resource cost.

The reality is that this section includes work already done, with information collated from any brief overview plan and subsequent review of the actual costs incurred through a pilot scheme or company operated scheme.

The added benefit of this section is that you will transfer the assumed costs into the next section of the plan.

Financial Projections

Opinion is divided on the optimal level of financial information. It depends on the target audience for your plan. For example, if you want to use the plan to secure a facility with the bank or external investors, then it is normal to include some historic figures if they are available, to show the actual profitability achieved, and then two, three or five years going forward.

I tailor the financial projections that I create to the target audience and so if a venture capital company has a five-year plan then the projections should reflect that term, even if the reality is that they will probably exit in three and constant monitoring and development over a period of time will show a variance in the figures two years into the life of the venture.

My advice to clients is to focus on a maximum of three years of projections initially, especially if it is a new venture. The reason for this is that the first year or trading is the important timescale and with actual historic figures a revised set of projections is far more beneficial to a strategic plan. Remember that a plan is only useful if it is constantly referred to and adapted as you go. If it is going to stay in a drawer then there is little point in spending time on it at all.

Often this section is a review of the basic work already carried out, as covered in Chapter 11, with any adjustment to the figures after all of the previous sections covered in this Chapter have been considered.

The aim of this section is to present the headline figures, with a brief narrative for each cost and any cross-reference to detailed calculations that may be an appendix to the plan. Profit and loss, balance sheet and cash forecast are an investor's main requirements.

Accurate figures and achievable results are essential to ensure motivation for key personnel who are involved in the plan and venture.

Evaluating the Plan

You may think that you have finished the plan once the previous sections are complete. However, there is one more section and it is probably the most important section: the management team's evaluation of the plan.

This evaluation is equivalent to a book-reading exercise, with everyone absorbing the plan from the first to last page. Arranging a meeting with everyone involved is the best way to encourage a team buy-in to the plan. The opinions and ideas offered at this meeting may lead to alterations in some parts of the plan. This is healthy, even if you have several meetings to review the amended plan until the final draft is completed.

A good idea is to work out some ratios based on the final financial information. Ratios are effectively snapshot figures for margin, return on investment or other values that banks and investors use. They are easy to work out with knowledge of fractions as long as you know where to look on a profit and loss, balance sheet or cash forecast. Although not imperative, knowing how they are calculated is useful if a finance person asks you for them. I have listed the main ones below.

- Gross Margin $= \dfrac{\text{Gross Profit}}{\text{Revenues}}$

  The most common ratio used by companies to gauge the performance trends, and perhaps to compare with a competitor.

- Return on Sales $= \dfrac{\text{Net Profit}}{\text{Revenues}}$

  Very similar to Gross Margin but this ratio includes the overheads, such as rent, salaries or administration costs, so that a true picture emerges. Again, this is a good ratio to analyse over time to see the trend.

- Return on Investment $= \dfrac{\text{Net Profit}}{\text{Equity} + \text{Debt}}$

  This shows, in percentage terms, how much the shareholders' equity and any borrowing equates to. The higher the percentage the better, and in layman's terms if the ROI gradually increases then the profits are increasing and / or the debt is reducing if the shareholders' funds are static. If it is decreasing there is something of a concern unless the company has borrowed for a new venture, say.

- Return on Equity $= \dfrac{\text{Net Profit}}{\text{Equity}}$

  This is similar to ROI but this ratio ignores debt and concentrates on the return for the shareholders. Some use this as a calculation for dividends in very basic terms, so with 20% ROE shareholders receive circa 20p for every £1 share. Of course this is a simple calculation and is unlikely, especially with taxes and / or the need to retain reserves for future investment.

Plotting these ratios over a period also highlights any big jumps or drops that require some investigation to find a valid reason. If none is found, then there might be something wrong with the financial projections.

Once you have completed a strategic document it will help guide you through a considered and rationalised development of your business. From this final document, it is very easy to write an operational version, which is more specific to the actual implementation of the programmes and strategies developed.

If you want further reading then seek out a copy of Lee E Hargrave's book "Plan for Profitability – How to Write a Strategic Business Plan". It is a great example of how to write a business plan.

Developing a strategic plan might seem like a mammoth task but like a journey take small steps to reach the end. If someone stops then they will definitely not finish the journey but if they find an easier downhill section then the steps get bigger and the finish gets closer. Some people don't want to take the journey alone, so take a guide who can help you reach the end quickly and safely!

I have my plan – Anything else before I boldly go where plenty have gone before?

To be completely candid here, there are so many unique factors it would take years to come up with a definitive list and this book would be akin to War and Peace.

The next chapter is a collection of considerations a little like this week's top ten; it could change next week if a really juicy consideration became the latest big thing.

13

Help!

I'm not sure I Can Do This

What if? Then they might? – Oh, and another thing!

Who knows best? – Ongoing Professional Development Advice

The assistance an experienced consultant provides can save you time and money; however some business people prefer to use their own experience, which is absolutely fine if that is the decision.

Overcoming problems, finding the answer or seeking out the answers using books just like this one, is a drug for some people. In some way that is why I wrote the book – so that answers are available. However, the book is an overview and it is impossible to cover every eventuality, which is why contracting a consultant is a cost-effective option for a lot of businesses considering franchising.

This chapter covers the standard considerations and tasks needed to launch a franchise. The headline "to do" list was covered in writing the strategic plan, but this chapter outlines a number of considerations and some tips that I hope are useful. The sub-headings reflect the usual areas of interest, which are often posed as questions; somewhere in the text is an answer or two.

How do I get a list together? – Come in mission control

With a strategic plan written, buy-in from existing staff and a commitment to go to launch capability, the countdown clock can start. However, just as at NASA, while the clock ticks down it is not unusual for doubt to creep in, even while systems are checked over and over again and all appears good. This is where the support team, including the consultant, can help put your mind at rest. The same philosophy applies for any franchise launch as occurs in a space mission. The rocket may have cleared the launch pad but keeping an eye on the instruments and gauges is fundamental to the success of the mission.

Until now the pre-launch planning revolved around the need to test the concept and thereafter to prepare to recruit able-bodied franchisees. You have used your business acumen and mapped the process to this stage, or you may have used a franchise-savvy consultant to help you prepare for launch.

The next stage, therefore, may or may not require further assistance. What is important is that the imminent launch needs a further review as you prepare to promote your business at franchise exhibitions, in magazines and newspapers, or on the internet. This is part of the operational plan that has evolved from the strategic plan exercise covered in the last chapter.

With advertising costs and a budget set, the focus moves to copy dates and allocating adequate time to designs and content so as not to delay the launch.

The short list of items is ...

- Staff the venture
- Have the agreement ready
- Market the opportunity
- Anything else before I hit the ignition switch?

Without further ado, let's look at each section in turn, with sub-headings for typical questions.

Pay nuts get monkeys – The importance of quality franchise-savvy staff

The analysis of the resources required includes the transition of employees ready to assume roles in the new support network, or the plan might have dictated the recruitment of new staff members for various roles. It is often decided to delay recruiting staff: why pay people to sit around while you attract and recruit new franchisees?

This is the way that new and fledgling franchisees often start. Commercially it seems a better financial decision, especially with the heavy investment already made to the project. If this is the preferred option and you have employees for the company operation then utilising the resource to show depth in numbers demonstrates a strong support function when potential franchisees attend for meetings and also provides them with an opportunity to interact with the support team, even if it is only a brief introduction during an office tour.

Employing people is a skill that we all learn over time, spotting the potential stars and identifying the work horses as well as the wasters! I have always adopted the philosophy that it is better to recruit someone who is better in a particular field than I may be so that they can assume autonomy and save me the time of doing their job for them as well as my own. Many senior executives deem this policy to be a potential threat to their own position, but it need not be. It's called team building, and if the employees are chosen carefully their aspirations will be clear. They will be happy in their own comfort zone and have no desire to take the Managing Director's office keys, not yet at least! For me it has worked in a number of businesses and has allowed me to concentrate on the plan, delegating tasks and liaising with the stakeholders. It has probably made it easier for some of those businesses to bring a "cheaper leader" in on at least one occasion – time for a change Chris! Perhaps on reflection I should have made myself bullet-proof and impossible to replace, but that would probably have made my day long and unproductive. Anyway, change is good and ethically I can honestly say that the businesses in my past lives have been stronger for this approach.

Why not just employ my neighbour?
He might be cheap.

This leads nicely into the section and my hope that your new franchise, or even existing business in need of a push, adopts a similar approach and methodology. Franchise-savvy staff will help you overcome the transition from standard business to the new franchise concept; they will understand the limitations of control with a contracted partner compared to employee, and the need for a firm but fair approach, which lies between customer service levels and employee relations. For many, it is truly a difficult level to understand. For example: how far should one go when faced with a debacle from a disgruntled franchisee?

Much the same as in any industry specialist careers evolve within the industry. Medical equipment sales people often move within the small number of manufacturers, advertising sales people move from A to B regularly and franchise-savvy staff move from concept to concept to further their career or for geographical reasons, to name but two.

This in turn has created specialist recruitment, offered as an additional service by consultancy firms working in franchising.

Where do I find these franchise veterans?

Iain Martin has been at the forefront of executive recruitment for many years with Kyros and latterly with The Franchising Centre, along with Brian Duckett. They also seek and place all levels of support staff in business development roles and provide commercial assistance.

They are not alone though. Franchise Development Services www.fdsfranchise.com also offers a similar service through Nick Williams and other regional advisors.

You may wonder why I have included my own competitors in this book. The answer is simple: they offer a great recruitment service and you deserve to have the links if you are serious about getting quality candidates.

Executives Online www.executivesonline.com is a great concept, providing interim placements as well as permanent positions. With an international presence via a franchised global network, they seek to find and secure suitable candidates for executive roles quickly. The business was set up by Norrie Johnson a few years ago, and more recently Anne Beitel has taken over as managing director. With a preselected database of interim and permanent candidates, they can place and fulfil the brief in a matter of weeks compared to the lengthy process of advertising a position, interviewing and then having to wait for the successful candidate to work a notice period.

Standard recruitment firms are useful in finding administration staff and can often find candidates who may have some experience in franchising. Having a franchise savvy staff member train the junior members of the team is the best option. Using a specialist middle manager who can educate employees will save on your time, unless the plan is for you to oversee the team training anyway.

No matter what recruitment firm you decide to use, remember that it is also important that any franchise veteran can adapt to new thinking. Franchising has evolved and continues to develop, indeed your concept may be new and exciting compared to the historic and established concepts, and therefore old methods might not fit very well. Echoes of "I used to do it this way" can haunt you if they are repeated on a daily basis.

Who is the right candidate? What should I look for?

Your business is important and you need time so that you can concentrate on developing the business. It therefore makes sense to employ the best individuals possible, within budget limitations, so that you let people do their job and avoid the age old problem of doing their job for them!

I have always sought people with three qualities above all of the rest. The first quality is being hungry for advancement, which is common, but when the second quality is sought it becomes rare. This second quality is common sense, which by definition is a combination of many other similar qualities, i.e. the ability to keep calm, be pragmatic and have the ability to resolve a problem. The final requirement is someone who is a good communicator because this is probably the most important attribute to have in franchising. Franchisees need confidence in the franchisor but if someone cannot communicate well and resolve problems quickly the problems can escalate and an employee will lose that trust. Once lost, trust is incredibly difficult to rebuild and that employee usually ends up in an untenable position.

Qualifications are important but not essential. There is no point in having a bookworm with the ability to sit and regurgitate a text book in exam conditions if they cannot use the knowledge gained in a practical situation. This is where common sense far outweighs any grade attained in a traditional educational establishment. I realise this is contentious, however given the choice to employ a graduate with a first class honours degree who cannot communicate or lacks common sense versus a person who has vocational qualifications or has implemented methods learned from books such as this one in a real situation, the choice for me is an easy one.

Applying lessons learned is what makes something happen and adapting theoretical methods to situations in an effective way is what makes a successful manager. Ideally this attribute is evident when you read through a pile of application forms and curricula vitae. Managerial qualities are evidenced by achievements in previous jobs.

Such a long list of criteria make it is difficult to find the ideal candidates, but they are out there.

How much should I pay? – Biting the salary bullet

I have indicated that "paying peanuts gets monkeys", a cliché that is so true. Saving a few pounds to get a body that may appear capable but has a missing link between brain and bodily functions will no doubt cost the business more in lost productivity and errors over time.

Advertising a position for say £20,000 and securing the right person for £21,000 is not a difficult decision. Indeed if they are hungry and even over-qualified, negotiating a starting salary with a guaranteed increase on completion of a probation period works very well. If you offer £20,000 a year with an increase to £22,000 after six months it is the same as paying £21,000 for the first year.

It takes time to recruit people, from advertising the position to the first day at work, so you have to take that into account when launching a franchise business. Timing is crucial so that people are not sitting around costing you money or you realise you have franchisees booked on training courses with no staff to accommodate them.

Seek out candidates that have experience and common sense above all. If getting the right person costs a few more pounds it is often better to invest in that individual instead of losing them and eventually employing a candidate who may be less able. Keep employees keen and motivate

Belt and braces – Investing in a fair but firm franchise agreement

This may seem a little late in the launch process but as in recruiting staff, the franchise agreement only needs to be ready when the business is ready to sell an area to an actual person.

How long will a franchise agreement take to complete?

Franchise agreements are fairly standard and the one your business finally uses will most likely be a hybrid version of the firm's blank agreement that complies with the latest legislation or guidelines from the bfa. An agreement should only take a few weeks to customise after an initial meeting with a legal advisor to ascertain the specific parameters within which the franchise intends to operate, such as area definition, training package offered, and limitations on buying supplies. A specific agreement also includes the franchise fee, licence fee and any specific requirements like uniforms. Too many businesses with new concepts have invested in an agreement by paying out at least £5,000 straight away only to incur further costs a year later to update the agreement after considering the pilot scheme or changes in legislation. This is why leaving the final agreement to the last moment may save you money.

Where do I start?

There are a number of franchise lawyers available and you will find a list of bfa accredited firms on the web site at www.bfa. org.uk

Having a good firm draft your agreement also helps to portray the professional image that in my opinion is essential. It shows your commitment to a fair but firm agreement and that although you are new to the franchise industry you are a serious player.

Always use a franchise lawyer to write your agreement and allow three to four weeks for a lawyer to write your bespoke agreement.

Write a list of important specific requirements that you want and let the lawyer draft the clauses.

Do you like my style? – Get the image and branding right

Converting a good idea into a saleable franchise concept requires a great image for the products or services offered as well as a great image of a real business opportunity for potential franchisees.

The best way to convey an image of great products or service is through concise text and good photography. Getting a digital camera and standing outside your premises clicking away may give you pictures, but not good images. The same is true for product shots and products in use; the 12 megapixel from Tesco will give you a picture but a photographer will give you a well lit image that you can use in literature and websites.

An advertisement or brochure using pictures that look cheap damages your image and brand.

Use a professional studio, like I Heart Studios, a modern creative business that can bring pictures to life and add creativity to the most mundane products. Photo shoots with proper backdrops and lighting are worth every penny. You can send boxes of products to the studio and receive the product back with a disc of amazing images that you can insert into your own documents, give to a designer to insert into literature, or a web designer for your website.

> Image is everything in franchising and this applies from the logo to the individual franchisees dealing with customers in a standard presentable manner, which might include uniforms or corporate clothing.

What makes a good logo?

Even if you have a logo already it is a good idea to look at alternatives to rebrand prior to launching the franchise. Often businesses that convert from mainline supply to franchising have a logo that is dated or doesn't portray the bigger image.

With the dramatic advances in computer graphics and the easier application of multi-colour vinyl vehicle graphics over the last decade, the constraints of one or two-colour multi-layer logos in a few fonts are thankfully behind us. The white van with a few words is also a distant memory and many mobile franchises now have full vehicle graphics with images of happy customers and franchisees, beautiful and clever.

What about a website?

Today, the web site probably provides the most important image. Even a small sole trader can give the impression of a global player through an effective website.

People have very different ideas of what makes a good web site. Some like flash images with a busy and fast-moving site that blows the visitor's socks off, while others prefer a site with concise salient information that loads quickly no matter what the speed of the broadband connection. What is abundantly clear is that you will not impress everyone who views your web site.

Where do I buy a domain?

Securing a domain for the franchise is fairly easy with the help of a web designer, or by searching on sites such as www.123-reg.co.uk where a dot com or dot co.uk will cost you less than £50 for two years.

Quick tip – ensure that you own the domain and it isn't registered with the web designer. This makes transfer to a different host much easier and any value in the domain is secure. 123-Reg and similar sites offer these derivatives of the dot com style, you can quite easily spend hundreds of pounds buying additional dot info or dot biz extensions of your chosen name.

Companies are formed every day with a descriptive name that says exactly what the company does, others have initials and some have only one word. Converting your company name to a suitable domain often means using lots of characters because the initials are already taken. For example Archive File Management UK missed out on www.afm.co.uk and so the only option was www.archivefilemanagement.co.uk

This is fine and it doesn't make a huge difference if people click their mouse on a web link on a search engine, such as Google, but www.afm.co.uk would have been ideal when quoting a web address over the phone or, more applicably, quoting an email address. For John West and AFM the domain name registered is only a portal and the information about the excellent cost savings for legal and education establishments is contained on the website.

Who should I get to build my site?

Although it is tempting to save thousands of pounds by building your own site, consider this only if you are an exceptional amateur web designer. There are some very good software packages and online instant sites available that require very little knowledge, but the finished article can look dated simply because web design technology is moving so fast that the "do it yourself" options are last year's methods.

Professional web designers are constantly looking for new technology and design improvements to build incredible sites for clients, which is where using a professional is a preferred option for most businesses.

The actual web design will require considerable input from you, because you must agree to the visible written content, irrespective of the web designer's image creation and code generation.

In reality, web designers are similar to architects who draft plans, discuss the plans with the clients and then revise the plans before submitting them for planning approval. Web designers collate information contained in your company literature and draft the wording, adding images and creating a layout; after you have reviewed and finally approved the text and layout, the web designer will complete the work and publish the site. If you are struggling to write text to give to the web designer then using the services of a PR agency is a good idea, or you can look at other franchise companies and what they include in their sites.

Try to include the salient sections with a simple but effective first page, information about you and your history and, of course, product information.

Testimonials from customers are another great addition to any site and if you commission a site that lets you amend your text so that you can add links to articles as you go it will save you money later, compared to paying a web company to update the site.

I could go on for pages but here is the thing; my idea of a good web site is purely personal, your idea may be very different.

Take advice from a web designer and make sure that they explain the latest technological advances so that your web site does not date quickly. There are ways to get your site to the top of search engines, using key words and optimisation, but they inevitably cost money; make sure you understand the method used and the ongoing cost to maintain a prime position. I find that a link to a well known portal is a simple but effective way to get traffic from anyone browsing "franchising" and enhancing your business.

What else is important for my site?

It has often been said that success in any business is not always based on better prices or even products but is earned through a good customer experience and the initial image portrayed.

The first impression must be of an exciting but professional franchise company. The prime objective is to generate enquiries from potential franchisees.

It is easy to confuse franchise recruitment and main marketing of products and services; however they are both in the same category and require equal attention because franchisees want the site to help them get new business.

How much information should I include?

Franchisees benefit from point-of-sale literature to help them secure business; this can be a multitude of computer-driven forms, proposals, data sheets or PDF brochures that they can use in email marketing campaigns. Including examples of sales brochures, testimonials, data sheets or franchise prospectuses sends a very clear message that you are serious and provide all of the paper and electronic tools needed to help your franchisees succeed.

Some franchisors prefer to keep the electronic literature out of the public domain in case a competitor gets hold of it or an individual decides to go it alone instead of pursuing a franchise route and therefore copies your literature. In reality, anyone who wants to get hold of a brochure or steal an idea will find a way, so why not show a potential franchisee what fantastic marketing tools you provide?

What about an online brochure?

Bespoke recruitment literature follows a fairly similar format for every company in the franchise arena. People want information and the opportunity to digest and compare this information in the comfort of their own home.

Providing a PDF version of the prospectus can help you get your information right into someone's home at the click of a button, preferably in return for an email address or telephone number.

Unfortunately there are a few comedians who claim to have Michael Mouse as their name, reside in Toon Town, Magic Kingdom, Orlando and an email address mickeyandminnie@ fairydust.something. I have even seen a business name like Countdown Cabs with a telephone number 9-8-7-6-5-4-3-2-1! There is no real way around this unless you decide to employ a system that captures the email submitted and the server sends the brochure to that email address instead of allowing a download immediately. This ensures that the person submitting the data cannot submit a fictitious email address. This doesn't prevent incorrect telephone or addresses being submitted. You must appreciate that there are people who don't want to provide you with information because they are cautious or don't want to be contacted yet. If people want to contact you then they normally release a number or email address when they are ready. Therefore why not let anyone download the information, even if a few prefer to leave fictional contact details?

What is a good prospectus?

Although I am sure many franchisors lay claim to the common style of innovative brochures available today, it is fair to say that literature has evolved over time.

The best ideas introduced over the last twenty years are now found in most franchise prospectuses. With similar text in almost every prospectus, you are judged on the quality of the brochure and unique information relevant to your business. A prospectus that is cheap and nasty will find its way to the "rejected" pile faster, as will one with an uninteresting company profile.

Inevitably franchise companies regularly pinch ideas from other franchisors in their attempt to have the latest idea and keep their literature fresh and exciting.

I suppose that this is good for franchising because the standard of literature improves every year.

A project to create a new prospectus can last months and the finished brochure is bound to include something that was seen in another piece of literature.

When I was working with ChemEx as Franchise Liaison Manager in my formative franchise years during the late 1990s, the Managing Director, Steve Bignell, and Chairman, Les Gray, spent months on a new style multi-page information pack destined to replace the historic collection of single pages. Working with Megan Dunmore PR and Paul Hathaway Designs, the first, second and third drafts included sections on common questions, profit examples and what to look for in a business. Some many thousand pounds later the brochures appeared at the next franchise show. At the next exhibition other franchise companies had new literature, but we had the jump on them and were already looking to a revised version.

To summarise, when you are designing you own prospectus or brochure it is totally acceptable to have a design that is similar to another company's material, but you must enthuse about your business to maintain identity and show the reader what a fabulous business you have, and how they can be a part of it.

How do I stop people copying my ideas?

The simple answer is you will not prevent another franchise company from copying a layout or even an innovative route to market. The important thing is to capitalise on this new way and then look for another way to replace it.

This can be a combination of new ways to exhibit with older literature or traditional ways to exhibit with new literature. Make the most of what you have and make it work.

In 1999 ChemEx made a real impression at the London franchise exhibition in Wembley. That was the era of the now legendary live "ChemEx Presentations" with a strong message bellowing out every half an hour over the three days. Crowds gathered for the performances, which by the third day were well rehearsed, to say the least. With the old guard Steve Bignell, Les Gray and Roger Wild positioned at the back of the crowd and business development managers Gary Allard and Niall Grange on the flanks, as soon as the presentation ended we pounced on people to give them information and steered them onto the stand for a more detailed discussion. By the end of the first day my script had been replaced with a fluent ad lib over a PowerPoint presentation. The initial annoyance of neighbouring stands turned to camaraderie by Sunday with regular name checks, and sincere thanks to our neighbours were broadcast to the crowds.

I was hoarse by the Sunday afternoon but it was worth it as that show generated lots of leads and eventually more franchisees than anticipated over the following six months. We made an impression with old literature and a dramatic presentation, although by today's standards it was fairly basic.

The new literature mentioned in the last section was ready for the next exhibition held in Birmingham in the autumn, and this new information combined with the regular presentations proved another hit with attendees.

At the following international franchise exhibition in Wembley in 2000, many companies had new information packs in a similar style and unsurprisingly around six companies had live presentations, which posed a problem for David Tuck of Venture Marketing. The noise level was reminiscent of a fairground, with everyone trying to compete in a decibel war.

I doubt if any of the other franchisors had ever picked up a radio microphone before and so when lots of microphones were set to similar frequencies it was hilarious to see some very confused faces as an alien voice from another stand started to resonate from their speakers. Despite the complaints about the noise and the channel confusion with the microphones, other companies caught the presentation bug and the following year some twenty live microphones appeared. That was when we decided that it was probably best to move on to something else. We had made an impression and the ChemEx presentations from the last century are now confined to franchise folklore.

This is why adopting a proven style is completely acceptable; copying word for word is not encouraged though.

I mentioned earlier the cost factor for literature and the timing of committing to print design and print run costs. It makes sense to have literature designed to a point that is almost print ready, but hold off on the print order until the last minute so that any final changes to information can be entered.

A month is usually enough time to agree a final proof and take delivery of the stock. It also makes sense to have a low print run; although this was more expensive per item historically, the advent of digital print has brought the cost down for small-print runs. You can easily reinvent and adapt literature after you have franchisees on board who can reinforce the wonderful message if you don't have 5,000 old copies in the storage cupboard.

Working backwards from your launch date certainly leaves time to work on content and design, perhaps even rebranding to a new logo. It also leaves time for trademark registration.

What do I wear to meet potential franchisees?

I started this section talking about image and you should consider, if only for a few seconds, your dress code.

Meeting franchisees comes later, after launch, but setting a policy depends on what type of business a franchisee is going to buy from you.

Things have changed quite a lot over the last few years and today people wearing suits often feel over dressed and perhaps threatening to people in the workplace and at exhibitions. Contrary to historic dress code thinking, it is now normal to see veterans of franchising adorned with open necked shirts, perhaps with embroidered logos on the breast pocket or even, shock horror, polo shirts.

Wearing a collar and tie is perceived as old style, but for me a mix of both is still important and it very much depends on the type of franchise. A white collar franchise that targets customers may still expect a collar and tie. A more relaxed white collar franchise, or one that adopts a more casual approach to business, justifies a casual approach from the franchisor as well.

Putting employees in uniforms or casual corporate attire is also a good idea and instigating this policy before launch is advisable. Should there be some resistance, get people used to change and avoid wasting valuable time debating the dress code at the crucial launch time.

There are plenty of good quality clothes that can be embroidered. Business attire used to consist of a suit, shirt and tie for men and dress or blouse with a skirt for women. This has now changed, with more businesses every year adopting casual attire: open neck shirts, polo shirts and chinos. More and more franchises now provide custom clothing for franchisees and employees, which in turn has also been identified as a franchise opportunity. EmbroidMe, launched by the Signarama outfit some years ago, is one of the fastest growing US franchises and one that is available in the UK and Europe now to cater for a growing demand for custom clothing.

Franchisees expect the full package, whatever that is, and so combining literature, image, brand awareness and a great first impression is essential if you want to stand out from the crowd.

Creating the right impression is a combination of good literature, a user friendly website and accessible information. Don't try to do everything yourself, use designers and advisors for the bulk of the work while ensuring that your business retains its unique identity.

14

Extra, Extra Read All About It

Launching Your Business

D-Day or is it L-Day? Either way here we go!

Before I start – Pre-launch promotion

After months of preparation your business is almost ready to
start selling franchise areas and with a target launch date
set the final pieces of the jigsaw include the fiddly bits, which
are the marketing, promotion and advertising shapes that interlock and fill the gaps.

When I refer to a launch date it sounds a little clinical. A
launch is normally when you are ready to proceed and more
often than not it is reactionary and not confined to a particular
date. Loosely speaking, most new franchise companies need a
level of promotion to announce to the world that they are open
for business and a definite date is a luxury.

I have mentioned web portals before in Chapter Two and some
rely on bfa membership to ensure that you are playing by the
association's rules whereas others do not require this membership. There are plenty to choose from and each one is designed
to direct traffic to your new website and generate new leads.

Advertorial styles

It may be that a launch date coincides with a franchise show or
with some articles commissioned. Therefore careful planning is
required to ensure that advertising copy is ready in good time
for publishers' final copy dates. In all cases, even if you are
launching a new franchise, it is far better to use past tense

instead of future tense. This style of writing will not date, whereas future tense not only dates but gives the impression of an inexperienced franchisor. I often refer to the ideal being "telling whilst selling" and it takes a little bit of practice to get a good story that shows real people in your environment compared to a "feature and benefit dump" in a few words.

Much the same as the interview with a potential franchisee, the best way to explain something is to use examples of others who have already decided to take the leap of franchise faith. This style works well for articles that are written for your wonderful business.

Someone that I have a great respect for, a mentor with whom I briefly had the pleasure of working in my short time with Signarama, was a great believer in the story-telling approach. Gary Lengel was the Executive Vice President and always had an uncanny gift of putting people at ease if they had a concern by using an example from his many years in franchising to explain how someone else overcame a similar barrier. Apart from the fact that he was a fabulous relaxed communicator, this approach won people over time and again, which is why Gary was so good at what he did.

The same approach to writing and creating advertisements and articles is very much part of my own armoury today. This book is littered with real examples and people to reinforce the thought process, although the people mentioned in the numerous examples may mean nothing to you. It does not matter, but using the method to explain that a real person did this or that is a great way of adding a human factor to a story. Using the pilot franchisee as an example of what the reader can achieve is far better than explaining what the business does and what the market may be. Writing an article about a franchisee's typical day should put the reader in their shoes, albeit briefly. Compare that to a plethora of facts and figures about the total market potential and earning potential.

Combining the two is ideal, of course. For example, by saying "Chris had his first appointment at 9.00 a.m. and visited a restaurant, one of the 30 he supplies out of around 300 in his area" instantly paints a picture of a reasonable start time for the day with 10% of the restaurants in the area already customers and 270 still potential customers. You could say "there are around 300 restaurants that can use your products and with say 30 you will have a great business", but which version sounds better? I will leave that one for you to decide.

Of course you will not have many, if any, real examples before you launch but there will be something to use, maybe the pilot scheme or the evolution of the business from a really successful company-owned operation to the new franchise concept.

Get help if you need it!

You either enjoy writing or you don't. More importantly, you might enjoy writing but people may not enjoy, relate to, or understand what you write. Of course it makes perfect sense to you, but consider that it might be a load of waffle. In fact you may consider this book in the same category, but if you do and have persevered to here then congratulations and thanks for reading it.

Let us consider that you have a great story to tell but don't know where to start. Picking up the franchise magazines and reading what other companies write about may give you an idea that could be the only start you need to draft your first article.

On the other hand, the franchise consultant can help you draft a few good articles or at least know someone who can.

The third option is to get some help from the franchise magazines that will be very keen to secure an order for some advertising space.

Designing advertisements is an art. Some prefer to pack information into a small box whilst others like to use visual methods to draw the reader into the select few words of dynamic text. Using someone to design an advertisement is probably the best idea and the creative juices can often deliver a great combination from the brief given. It may cost a few hundred pounds, even a thousand, but you will have artwork ready to send to magazines. Franchise World, as indeed other specific magazines, can create an advertisement for you from a logo and some text. Decide on the level of advertising and target the publications that you wish to use, write the articles and design the advertisement and get everything ready in good time for copy dates, which are often a good few weeks before publication. Work backwards and ensure you have adequate time.

Write about real people and real experiences; don't be afraid to address common concerns and how to overcome problems.

Try to engage with the readers and make the article about them, not all about you!

Here we go – Going to market

With articles written, advertisements designed, proof signed off, and copy in place, launching your franchise business used to depend on the magazine hitting the newsstands. Not today though. The printed material is not the driver for launch date. Signing up to web sites is quick and less time critical.

All the preparation in the world is worthless unless you are ready to take calls.

Your franchise could be open to the planet within hours from paying your money to the web site host by credit card.

Whether you are waiting for a publication date for a magazine or you have a presence on a franchise web portal, the day that your business is actively advertising you must be ready to take calls and start selling your fabulous business.

We are ready – Making sure that you are geared up to take enquiries properly

One of the biggest mistakes that franchisors make when launching their business is the way that they handle enquiries from potential franchisees. After spending a substantial amount on research, consultancy fees, marketing, brand design and resources, they often open for business and make a complete hash of the first impression.

Remember that potential franchisees are looking for a warm and informed first impression. They are seeking a company that sounds professional and a family that will welcome them in.

The best way to ensure that your business makes a good impression is to provide the proper training to anyone who may answer a call or reply to an email. Communications policies may sound grand but no matter what size your business is, maintaining a standard policy is the best way to get the right impression across.

Answering calls

Answering a telephone promptly is not a trade secret; many companies have operated that way for decades. Picking up the phone in three to five rings is now the norm. We can debate the benefit of call options, selecting one for sales and two for accounts followed by further options, until the cows come home. The benefits are direct contact with the department you wish to speak to but personally I think that it is so impersonal that it does not fit the franchising ethos. Franchising is a people business where franchisees buy into a concept from a person and in turn customers buy from franchisee people. Automating the first impression may be more cost effective, but it can be frustrating when you simply want to talk to someone. I don't know about you, but if I have to speak about a problem with a utilities supplier or any company, I would prefer that someone speaks to me without spending a minute or two waiting for the most relevant option, only to reach the wrong department or have a pre-recorded voice tell me that I am in a queue and that my call will be answered in five, four, three, or two minutes. Now imagine someone who has read about your fantastic opportunity and is so excited that they pick the phone up and dial the number only to be greeted with a multiple-option response.

Just as important is what is said, so any calls into the main line have to be answered in a professional manner with the company name, your name and an offer of assistance, e.g. "Newco, Chris speaking, how can I help you today?" You would be amazed how many people still answer the phone with "hello" or "yep", so make sure you start with a professional policy. These are the basics and I think we should move on to the crux of the advice before I write another page on how to answer the telephone.

Be prepared – no, not Scout's Honour

Right, call answered. The first piece of definitive advice is to make sure that the person answering has a pen and scribble pad next to their phone, asks the name of the caller as soon as possible in the conversation, and writes it down. After this they can refer to their notes during the conversation to ensure they use the correct name. This avoids the embarrassment of addressing Mr. Smith as Mr Fish, or Alan as Andy. Believe me, it is easy to do!

Not listening is the biggest mistake people make when conversing: if you do not listen you'll miss something.

How to handle questions

It is impossible to predict every question a caller is going to ask, which makes training and role playing a standard telephone call virtually impossible. However, it is possible to train someone to be receptive and maintain the objective to get a name, number, area and maybe an email address so that you can send more information and call to offer further help. You can role play this scenario and train someone to keep it simple, even if that is simply transferring the call to whoever is selling the franchise.

Typically, a potential franchisee wants the answer to three questions;

- Is there anyone in my area?
- How much is the franchise?
- How much can I earn?

In all cases, there is no need to offer an answer at all at this stage, which may seem a little strange. The call is merely the opportunity to speak to a real person who is interested in your business, so why risk losing any interest by informing them that there is another franchisee in the area they live in?

Standard answers, so that everyone says the same thing, are easily taught.

The following examples are the type of questions and standard answers that employees should practice and use when somebody calls.

- Area? – I don't actually deal with the territories but I know we have availability in your area.
- Cost? – Virgin territories start at (whatever) and we have other options that we can discuss with you at an informal meeting.
- Earnings? – Unlimited, you can build the business to whatever level you want. Again, we go through the figures during any subsequent meeting.

It is isn't always that easy and people will be persistent, in some cases demanding information. If this is the case, stop the conversation and promise a call-back.

The ability to read and research online is great for those that have access to the internet, but don't assume that everyone prefers to read a prospectus on line; offer a hard copy in the post.

Be careful – don't say too much

People want information and the temptation is to tell them everything to get them excited. The problem is that today people expect every conceivable answer, either in the body of a website or in a prospectus. If you do not give them the answers they become cautious, sceptical and may even think that you have something to hide. This age old dilemma is still faced by franchisors today, and will be next year and beyond. So just how much information is enough to gain interest?

Finding how much information is the optimum amount takes time, which is why the best way to find the optimum level is to have a dedicated person deal with all initial franchise enquiries.

If that person feels that releasing information about areas, profitability or whatever the question is will benefit the process, then the effectiveness of such decisions will be abundantly clear when you analyse the recruitment rates later.

Too much information can kill the sale at first contact, therefore training staff to maintain a standard set of answers is the best option.

Dealing with obnoxious people

In following a uniform policy there may be the occasional rude person who "demands" information and constantly tries to control any conversation, something reminiscent of a teenage debating club meeting.

People can be incredibly churlish on the telephone when they can hide behind a piece of plastic. They bring up the smallest of objections, perhaps to take some satisfaction out of bullying someone, or in a perverse way trying to catch them out and in turn make them feel uncomfortable. This is of course wrong, but it goes with the territory. The best option is to funnel these people politely to the team leader.

Over the years I have had my share of rude people and with

the luxury of choice that comes with running a franchise business it becomes an easy decision to simply cut a poor conversation off by telling someone that they don't have the right attributes to join the business.

This may appear an arrogant or defensive approach but if you speak to someone for 20 minutes and maintain a level of decorum throughout then it soon becomes clear when someone is a time waster and would be a thorn in your side if they were to sign up. If you have answered lots of normal questions, offered candour and really tried to be friendly to an individual who is still aggressive and rude there is nothing wrong in deciding to reject that person and save time for everyone.

Thankfully, most people just call to request basic information and so are "reaching out" to you and your business, testing you as a possible partner of the future.

If you handle the call with professionalism and courtesy there is no reason why you cannot achieve the aim of the first contact call – to get a mailing address and a contact telephone number.

Be prepared is the motto, answering the telephone is not difficult if your employees follow simple rules. The objective is always to get contact information or sell the benefit of meeting with the franchise team to tell them more and satisfy their thirst for information.

They have done it – Using success to generate PR stories

I have already mentioned the importance of generating real examples of people working a franchise system. This is a great tool to use when people start to contact you with an interest in your business so I have included a section at the end of this chapter as well.

Real people and real stories are very important, so remember to use stories that people can relate to at every opportunity as you start to talk to people and invite them to meetings to discuss the franchise in more detail.

As you start to recruit franchisees you will soon have even more opportunities to use new stories as long as you keep in touch with your franchisees and encourage open discussion. Take an interest in all franchisees and remember they are individuals as well as business partners. Make sure that regular calls are not pure question and answer sessions with a transparent goal to get information to help you sell franchises.

The best stories often develop over time. For example when a franchisee tells you that they approached a big account this is good, but not the complete story. However, if you find out a month later they have secured the business the story has a beginning and second chapter. If the franchisee continues to offer great service then the story can develop into a more powerful example.

Turning the franchisee's journey into a few choice words is similar to telling someone about what you did at the weekend. Keep it interesting and concise or you may bore the pants off someone. When you start to use and tell stories the ones that seem to work give you an inkling of which ones you can expand upon and consider for a written press release or article.

Creating articles inevitably involves the franchisee so make sure that if you do use information the customers are happy for you to name them, just in case they prefer anonymity. This is normally a formality as most businesses welcome positive publicity and by definition, success stories are positive for suppliers and customers alike.

The whole process is ongoing and if recorded properly a library of stories is one of the most powerful franchise sales tools available. The added benefit is the internal motivation for other franchisees with examples of what they can use to gain business from similar businesses.

Not all stories are about providing products or a service

Stories are not always about gaining business. They may be how a franchisee works with a local sports team and sponsors the team kit, as an example. It may be a charity event or recognition from an external body such as the local Chamber of Commerce. Another good subject is growth, where a franchisee shows commitment to the franchise and the potential by taking on a second area, a second retail outlet or more staff.

Some franchisors use awards to recognise sustained growth or the achievement of turnover thresholds and they present these awards at regional meetings or annual conventions. Recognition of achievement means very little to people outside the network but reaching a turnover level and receiving a plaque or framed certificate provides motivation and a photo opportunity for a story.

Using recognition awards by adding further levels, for example one star to five star awards, is another way of giving people a goal. Adding in Franchisee of the Year or recognising consistent achievement years later in a "Hall of Fame" may be over the top for some and incredibly American, but for me they are a great way of binding the franchisees together.

Maintaining good publicity requires effort and creativity. Write stories and include examples of successful franchisees to show what a great franchise business you have.

15

The Select Few

Signing up and Training Franchisees

Thanks for the cheque – now let's get you started!

On the dotted line please – How to sign people up and welcome them to your little family

Somewhere between the first advertisement and press release and signing your first franchisee you will make a critical decision with a potential franchisee to go ahead and sign up.

The various meetings and discussion around that critical decision follow a path, even if either the potential franchisee or the franchisor wanders off on what appears to be a shortcut to arrive about the same time at the destination. That destination is the signing hut at the end of the path. In that hut is a door that opens to the rest of their life which has a map showing the way for the next part of that person's life. This map is provided by the franchisor, however the franchisee decides which direction to take. Franchisors are merely tour guides to start with, and eventually trip advisors.

The path to the signing hut is perilous and at any time the travellers may run off into the woods never to be seen again, perhaps signing at another signing hut.

In case you missed the message let me clarify. Signing people up is never exactly the same for any two people. Each franchisee has specific questions and everyone has the potential to decide not to proceed at any point, even at the last minute with a pen poised over an agreement.

First Contact

I mentioned the importance of presenting a professional image to the potential franchisee at the first time call or contact.

Either the Managing Director or an appointed person has to take ownership of all enquires, however they are received. That person must ensure that email enquiries are answered, or calls returned in a timely manner. It is a good idea to go a stage further and pick up the telephone and introduce yourself and your interest to every potential franchisee, even if it is only an enquiry at this stage. If you decide to send a standard email response, it's a good policy to ensure a follow-up email or chase letter is sent a few days later.

First Conversation

By the first conversation I am referring to the first serious conversation that you have with a potential franchisee.

Answer questions briefly, but remember that you really want to arrange a meeting so that you can give more detailed answers whilst presenting information that cannot be visualised in a phone conversation.

Keep focused and be strong so that you do not say too much and confuse the subject when the message can be explained more clearly with a visual aid, such as a spreadsheet or information pack.

Resist the temptation to discuss availability of territories or prices until you have met the individual and found out about their circumstances.

The goal of the first conversation is to arrange a meeting, either at your premises or at a suitable location close to the enquirer's home. However, you must sell the time required for this meeting. Make sure that they are aware that you need an hour or two to fully explain or show them your business. Five minutes in a hotel lobby is useless.

Making an Appointment

The appointment is the crucial part of the recruitment process, therefore making the appointment is just as important.

Calling a potential franchisee after receiving a returned questionnaire contained in the prospectus pack that your team sent in the post, or a submitted version sent electronically, is a tried and tested method. If someone has taken the time to complete a form they are calling out to you to contact them and arrange a meeting. These forms are great and give you information prior to calling them so that you can tailor the discussion to the individual's concerns or circumstances – previous experience or financial constraints, for example.

Another good suggestion is to have a question asking for the best time is to call them back. If this is completed then make sure that you respond at the preferred time.

If nothing is entered remember that people are possibly at work and cannot talk during working hours. Calling someone in the evening shows that you work outside the nine-to-five stereotype of a business. Making a call on a Sunday night is another good option and in most cases people are receptive, even if it is a disruption to their home life. It is also a good time if they are facing the Sunday night blues when they start to think about having to go back to work in the morning, a job they perhaps don't like very much.

Keep the conversation concise and try to focus on the goal to meet with the candidate to answer questions. Try to avoid being lured into an hour-long telephone interview.

You may also sense whether the candidate is right for your business by their telephone manner but try not to throw the baby out with the bathwater! First contact calls can get off on the wrong foot, especially if the candidate is defensive and scared to show any form of commitment. Try to reserve judgment until you meet someone but remain steadfast that you need to meet to disclose sensitive information about your business.

Some candidates demand that you send everything you have before they will entertain a request for a meeting, which is not only rude but incredibly short-sighted. It really is up to you how you respond and might be based on how desperate you are to recruit franchisees. From experience, I assume that if someone is not prepared to meet up after an initial discussion unless I send names and addresses of every franchisee, and their family members, then they may not be a welcome addition to my little franchise family. End of conversation.

Where to meet

Opinions in the franchise fraternity are divided on where the first meeting should take place. This decision is really a luxury, or a quandary, to established franchise companies. A new franchise such as your business may only have a few widespread franchisees, if any at all, therefore making the effort to travel three hours north to meet someone is probably your best option.

It is a good idea to confirm an appointment the day before and you set off on a lengthy drive. There is nothing worse than rising with the lark and arriving at a hotel to meet someone only to turn around and head back south an hour later when they don't show up.

If you have a retail type of franchise, meeting someone close to one of your franchised stores is ideal so that you can meet and have a conversation before taking them to see a franchise in operation. This luxury is only feasible when you have a spread of franchisees around the country, as well as contented franchisees who are happy for you to bring people into their business and, more importantly, are positive about the business.

Structuring the first meeting

The goal of the first meeting is subject to ongoing debate in the franchise community. This debate stems from a belief, by some, that providing too much information has a detrimental effect on the informal sales process and actually turns people off from the potential with a massive information dump, a bit like a hard sell approach. Others believe that the information dump is critical to open discussion and that people expect to be told everything, to enable them to carry out research. All I can say is that in my experience, bombarding people with facts, figures and features associated with benefits has lost more candidates than it has won. The debate will no doubt continue for many years and so it is really personal, derived from experience and analysing the results.

Asking questions is the best approach as long as you listen to the answers and tailor stories to particular circumstances. For example if a potential franchisee comes from a particular background then if possible talk about the positive experiences of someone with a similar working history who is already in your network. Showing how a franchisee gained a good customer is a way of encouraging a potential franchisee to form a positive opinion of the sales process.

Calm concise questioning about home life and the candidate's financial needs provides a wealth of information. If someone needs £3000 a month to pay the mortgage and bills and you would expect that they may achieve this net profit in six months, then they need six months of savings otherwise they will probably fail. Remember, they are not buying a salary!

The ethical approach is the right approach although it is very tempting to take franchisees on, even if they have a high chance of failure, because of their personal attributes or financial position. This is your decision but having a high attrition of franchisees will damage your recruitment levels later and demotivate the network.

Keep the first meeting as informal as possible. Offer information verbally and in printed format and perhaps provide a copy of the franchise agreement along with a profit example. If you do offer this information then go through the profit example and explain the costs and income briefly, stressing that this is an example and that you expect franchisees to achieve above the conservative figures presented.

The franchise agreement should be explained briefly and it is best to concede that the legal format is needed to protect franchisees as well. It is often a good idea to look someone in the eye and tell them that the contract is standard and that you don't vary it for individuals. Suggest that they have it checked by a legal advisor and that they should expect to pay anything from £300–£1000 but that a local conveyance lawyer is not really a good option as they are not versed in franchise law. A better option is a franchise lawyer and these can be found on the bfa website.

The first meeting should be concluded informally; an explanation of the next step, or what you hope to achieve from a further meeting, is a good way to finish.

Suggest that they bring their life partner to the next meeting for you to meet as part of the selection process. Let the candidate know that it is a good idea to write questions down and bring the list to the next meeting. Also let them know that the next meeting will be more formal and you will discuss areas and training in more detail. In other words, structure a second meeting in their head, in advance.

The structure of the second meeting

The second meeting is more formal because both parties are seeking commitment. As franchisor you need to accept that the candidate is right for your business, so remember that very important point.

If the first meeting was not at the head office then the second definitely needs to be there. A tour of the facility is needed and perhaps a look at the map that shows where franchisees are already working, and even a scattering of people interested, represented by coloured dots. This is a very good visual aid that shows commitment already gained from candidates and franchisees. The psychological effect on a candidate is that they see others and are not alone in considering your business. The impact of seeing someone else interested in their preferred area triggers a "fear of loss" and can help you secure deals.

The goal of a second meeting

The aim of the second meeting is to gain commitment but the recruitment process is rarely a two-meeting process today, as it often was, say ten years ago.

Historically, people read and signed agreements without taking legal advice, which was fine until legislation changed and people had to be given the option of taking legal advice. If they waived this right that was fine, but the franchisor had to prove that the option had been offered; this led to a few test cases and loopholes when it was perceived that franchisees had not been duly informed and in a few cases the contract was deemed to be void. In agreements today, specific clauses are inserted that confirm the franchisee had been informed of the option of taking legal advice.

Occasionally potential franchisees want to talk to existing franchisees and it is a good idea to impose a policy that franchisees should not talk to candidates unless the meeting has been sanctioned by the franchisor. Why? Partly because competitors could pretend to be interested and canvass franchisees for operational secrets, prices, profit levels or even customer details so that they can attempt to poach them and partly because you don't want franchisees to receive lots of calls when they are building a business. This policy will protect your business and help you achieve higher recruitment levels.

Verbal commitment is often the best achievement you can expect after a second meeting; however pre-selling a deal with confirmation that there is agreement, subject to a positive report from a legal advisor, is totally acceptable.

Taking Deposits

Speeding up the recruitment process is difficult but there are methods that you can use to gain commitment.

Deposits are normally refundable although franchisors can justify withholding some of the deposit to recover costs incurred in, say, finding properties, as long as they state this in the deposit receipt issued. Deposits show commitment and person-ally, I believe that a refundable deposit is merely a psychologi-cal commitment. So why bother at all? You may well ask. The fact is that a refundable deposit is a good way of committing someone and it gives you an option to resell the concept if a refund is requested. If this does happen there is another chance to overcome objections and talk someone round if they get cold feet. On the face of it, refundable deposits also show a good level of confidence in your system.

There are occasions when people give you a refundable deposit and then disappear into the ether. Perhaps they have run off into the woods from the path to the signing hut! Another rare occurrence, but one that at least provides you with a little income to mitigate the time spent trying to recruit them. Maybe it is embarrassment or a fear that you will force them into sign-ing a contract or you will submit them to Chinese water torture. Who knows?

Requesting a deposit by cheque or bank transfer after the sec-ond meeting is a soft sell approach, allowing the candidate to go away and make a decision. It is a risk, but it gives you a reason to call after a few days to discuss a decision.

What is a suitable deposit? I would say between 10% and 20% of the total investment is a suitable figure. With the eighties, nineties and noughties now behind us, the subject of deposits is destined to be a discussion point well into the teenies, for that I am sure.

Signing the Contract – Closing the Deal

After two or maybe three meetings the final stage is to sign the contract. How exciting!

By now you will know quite a lot about your new franchisee and after an exchange of emails, possibly answering questions or fighting off the concerns raised by lawyers, this is perhaps the most satisfying meeting for franchisors.

Although it is a very important meeting it is often the most light-hearted and friendly meeting of all, submerged in positive discussion about training dates, and the exciting opportunity that lies ahead.

With contracts signed and the financial details arranged it is time to get ready for the induction of the latest family member.

Let's get on with it – Keeping in touch prior to training, bombarding them with information

The euphoria of signing a franchisee up is fantastic but the serious part is about to start. Now you have to deliver on your sales pitch and provide that franchisee with a return for their investment and a blueprint to create a successful business that sustains their income expectations.

There is usually a gap between signing and training although sometimes it may be only a few days if the franchisee is available for the next induction training course. Whatever the gap, it is a really good opportunity to help prepare for the pending launch of their business. Provide data sheets of key products or services so that they can familiarise themselves with actual information for the first time.

Finding the right location

Securing premises and helping with the lease negotiation is often a part of the service offered by a franchisor. This can be anything from finding a location for someone prior to the agreement being signed or pushing agents and landlords to expedite the lease quickly, after the event. Unfortunately the lease system in the UK is laborious and extremely time-consuming compared to the US where you can get someone into a location in a matter of weeks at worst under boiler plate agreements.

In the UK the usual timeframe is around twelve weeks, with searches, lease negotiations and remedial work required clogging the process beyond belief. Because of this it is wise to start looking as soon as possible and make an offer prior to signing otherwise your franchisee might be waiting months before they can start, which is disappointing for everyone.

This problem is eradicated if you sell an existing franchise, but again the transfer of lease can prove time-consuming.

Share a day with a franchisee

Spending a day with a franchisee is another way of filling time before the induction training course.

Prior to signing there is always a risk that spending a day with another franchisee might spook a potential franchisee. They may panic and decide that they "can't do it", which is a natural reaction with such a life-changing decision. Some franchisors therefore do not offer a day just in case they lose a candidate. If you do offer a day with a franchisee then make sure that they follow the system and demonstrate the way that you train someone.

Cross the "T's" and dot the "I's"

No matter what information you share prior to the induction training course, or how much involvement there is with a location negotiation, it is good to call your new family member regularly even if it is only to check on VAT registration, sizes for uniforms, address for stationery or a simple conversation to inform them of exiting news about a new national account for the network.

I think this is really important and starts the business relationship off properly.

Find an excuse to keep in contact with your new "sign up" even if it is the occasional call to let them know you are working on their pre-induction course checklist and cannot wait until they start

Follow the system – Creating a comprehensive operation manual

The Operations Manual should be finished at the very latest just before the first induction training course.

The time between signing up franchisees and that course is the ideal time to finish off the manual, version one that is, because you will need to update the manual as you go.

A good manual evolves over time, with new practices and procedures added or replacing the first version.

Collating the manual takes time, is somewhat laborious and is another task that a consultant will do for you if you prefer to farm the boring bit out!

The standard sections of a manual are as follows, these have various sub-headings or categories specific to your business as well as the usual "do's and don'ts";

1. Introduction
2. Manual Guide and Contents – table of contents and how to use the manual
3. The Company – background and who's who
4. Your Business – how the franchised business fits in to the market
5. Your Responsibilities – a gentle reminder of what you have to do
6. Territory Limitations – policy on borders and trading
7. Products and Services Available – the acceptable products or services offered, often a blanket statement that new products are added regularly
8. Clients/Customers – who they are and where to look for them
9. Standard Procedures – this section is only included if the franchise has a stringent procedure for, say, a site survey or consultation for which the law requires a particular stringent procedure
10. Health & Safety – confirmation of requirements for the business operation

11. Sales & Marketing – techniques methods and suggestions
12. Purchasing – approved suppliers, procedures and terms
13. Corporate Presentation – clothing, websites, livery store design and literature requirements
14. Office Administration – the standard procedures used
15. Accounting – how to keep records and comply with legislation
16. Licence Compliance – reporting requirements
17. Intellectual Property – confirmation of trademarks and ownership
18. Legislation – clarification of anything relevant to the business operation under the franchise banner

With approximately eighteen sections, each with sub-sections, it is not unusual to have over one hundred pages, which is why I have not provided a full example in this section.

Ideally, each subsection should appear on a separate sheet and the whole document should be contained in a sturdy file with an electronic copy on disc, or preloaded onto any hardware, included in the package.

The operations manual is the bible according to your business and is a collection of gospels from your own disciples. Let your people have an input to how things are done and the manual will benefit from this input.

Is everyone ready? – Making sure that your team is ready

The second countdown in your now *franchised* business is the induction training course date; the first was the launch date which seems years ago by now.

The size of the team depends entirely on your resources and requirements in your business plan. There might be only one person carrying out training and supporting the franchisees.

Whatever the number of team members, or even if there is only one person, there is a need to get ready for the induction training course and make sure that everything promised to the franchisee for their package is on schedule for delivery in advance.

The content of the induction course is covered in the next section but it's a good idea to write it and print off whatever copies are required prior to 9.00 a.m. Monday!

If you do have a team of people it is a good idea to sit down with everyone the day before the course starts and run through everybody's involvement and what they are presenting. A "dummy run" presented to someone not involved in the venture, such as a family member or friend, is a great way to boost confidence. Motivate the troops and get them excited about the course. If they enjoy the course your new franchisee or franchisees will as well.

Whether it is the first or fiftieth induction training course go through the checklist the day before to make sure that the salient information is printed off and that people involved know what they are doing.

Boring, boring, boring – Developing the induction training and getting the right mix

The aim of any induction course is to convey the important information in a constructive way. Franchise induction training courses evolve over time, so don't expect to get everything right first time and accept that reviewing and changing the format for the next course is best practice.

Student spotting

The unknown factor is the students. Everyone responds and soaks up the facts presented differently, but thankfully they fit into categories. In the first part of this book I mentioned the disruptive types that a franchisee may encounter during the training course. The advice for a franchisee is to recognise these types and concentrate on their business and quest for knowledge. This also applies to the franchisor, but controlling the characters so that they don't take over the course requires a firm hand and the occasional conversation in a separate room. If you handle a disruptive franchisee that has seen and done everything and cannot be taught anything new properly, they too will benefit from your course.

Identify individual characters so that you can control the course!

How long should the course be?

The best courses have two or more franchisees attending; however you might have a single franchisee for a new franchise. For some reason you do get through an agenda more quickly with one franchisee and the one-on-one tutorial sessions seem to go faster. This is why it is worth considering condensing a week-long course into three days and providing an alternative for the two remaining days, such as time with the pilot scheme franchisee or marketing with them in their area.

The length of any training course depends on how complex the franchise is, and how much information and detail a franchisee really needs to start trading. Too much and they will switch off, too little and they will struggle. As Big Brother's commentator said, "you decide".

There is no defined length but let us assume that for the following example the course is a week long, simply because most franchisors run five-day induction courses.

If your course is usually a week long then condense it down to three days if you have only one franchisee – a week is too long one to one!

An example of a course agenda

It is probably a good idea to follow an agenda that everyone is aware of on the first day of the induction course. To help you consider what is usual, a few explanatory words follow the example of daily activities. Some sections may not even apply to your business but the core activities will most definitely be appropriate.

Day One

8.30 a.m.	Collect Franchisees from Hotel
9.00 a.m.	Welcome and Introduction
9.30 a.m.	Overview of the Products or Service
10.30 a.m.	Coffee break
10.45 a.m.	Products/Service in detail Part One
12.30 p.m.	Buffet Lunch – Meet the Team
1.30 p.m.	Marketing Your Business

2.45 p.m.	Coffee break
3.00 p.m.	Products/Services Part Two
4.15 p.m.	Coffee break
4.30 p.m.	Round Up and Homework
4.45 p.m.	Drop Franchisees at the Hotel
Evening	Free Time for Franchisees

Collecting franchisees from a hotel on the first day at the very least avoids the prospect of waiting for people to arrive. Suggest that franchisees check into the hotel on a Sunday night to ensure they are not going to get stuck in traffic and delay the start of your carefully planned course.

The short drive to the training facility provides an opportunity to talk casually about things totally unrelated to the course, which is a great way to help them relax. It is like first day at school for a nervous child. Remember that.

The welcome and introduction session is another way of explaining the week in full whilst introducing time constraints and their importance to ensure a smoothly run course. If you have more than one franchisee then a round table introduction for each student is a great way of letting them say who they are and what they have done. You can add a question about what they are looking for from the course.

Present each attendee with their own copy of the operation manual, ensuring that they sign a receipt for the manual. This is the first administrative task but is a requirement to protect the business later and usually includes a statement that the signee acknowledges the manual remains the property of the franchisor and cannot be copied or given to anyone else. The statement usually includes notification that it is the franchisee's responsibility to update the copy when new versions are received.

With the formalities completed, get on with the first interesting bit to keep attention levels high. A detailed overview of the products or service for about an hour is a powerful way to start.

The first lunchtime is a good time to introduce members of the team to new franchisees in a very informal way.

After lunch start going through the products or service in more detail, adding nuggets of information and demonstrating what they do, and what is different from comparable competitors' products or services.

Winding up Day One

Remember that the first day is energy-sapping for everyone and although it might appear a short day compared to a full day at work, regular breaks are important to maintain attention levels.

Setting homework after reviewing the day is a good way of providing a task for the franchisees to complete in their own time that evening, which is why you let them have free time. If you have more than one franchisee, suggest they meet up for a drink before getting an early night after a mind-blowing day.

It is a good idea to remind franchisees that even though they are away from home it's probably wise not to overdo the alcohol consumption as hangovers don't mix well with a day in a classroom. Of course you need to explain that in a witty way, but with a hidden message.

Taking franchisees back to the hotel at the end of the day also allows you to seek opinion on how the first day went; buying a drink at the bar is another good way of bonding with franchisees before leaving them to their homework and some free time.

Day Two

8.00 a.m.	Meet Franchisees for Breakfast
8.45 a.m.	Bring to Training Room
9.00 a.m.	Review Day One
9.15 a.m.	Review Homework (Test)
9.30 a.m.	Administration – forms and systems
10.45 a.m.	Products/Services Part Three
12.30 p.m.	Buffet Lunch
1.30 p.m.	Introduction to Sales
2.45 p.m.	Coffee break
3.00 p.m.	Introduction to Sales Part Two
4.15 p.m.	Coffee break

4.30 p.m.	Round Up and Homework
4.45 p.m.	Drop Franchisees at the Hotel
Evening	Free Time for Franchisees

It is always a good idea to arrive at the hotel earlier on the second day and have breakfast with the franchisees before taking them to the training centre. Arranging for different team members to collect franchisees on different days also encourages a bonding between franchisees and individual employees.

Start promptly at 9.00 a.m. and review the first day before a quick informal test, which can be written or verbal.

It is a good idea to break down the administration section into small bite-size pieces and schedule them at different times of the day. Notwithstanding the importance of administration, it is a good idea to slot a product-oriented session before a buffet lunch.

Sales training – in a little more detail

Another section that scares some franchisees is the dreaded sales training. Depending on what a franchisee has done in their working life they may not consider themselves as a salesperson, which is why the introduction should emphasise the simplicity of sales.

Remember that franchisees are not employees and have bought a whole business, not a sales job, which is why it is important to ease them into sales techniques and avoid bombarding them with jargon.

Over many years of presenting sales training I have developed a system that is a hybrid version of many ideas and philosophies based around simple sales techniques, all designed to build franchisees' confidence. This system works for me but you may wish to consider alternatives based on your own experiences.

I start sales training by introducing franchisees to the concept of simple communication. Selling is about communicating and, most importantly, listening to a customer. Listening is exactly what we do in a social environment and without knowing it we sell ourselves every day when we meet new people. When you go to a party you are introduced to other people or you go over to introduce yourself to someone; when you do this you normally say who you are and how you know the host. After that you start asking questions and listening to the answers. From that encounter the person you are talking to will make a judgment on you as a person, whether they like you or not, and this is obvious by the way they respond to further conversation, or how comfortable they seem to be. This is what sales is all about; it is exactly the same as having a conversation with someone but with the added objective of selling a product or service. Without personal acceptance a sale is incredibly rare.

When you explain this to a franchisee who has not sold before, or should I say been employed as a salesperson because they will have sold themselves to others, they relax and absorb more of the training.

The good, the bad and the ugly

Using examples of poor sales techniques and highlighting good ones is a great way of introducing different ways of selling, perhaps subconsciously, before explaining body language and what to look for. I also explain the importance of making a good first impression.

The last part of my first sales session is an explanation of the different ways people close the sale: the direct ask, alternative close, sympathy close, price comparison close and the introductory offer close. At least this is what I call them, although I am sure that others use different names for exactly the same thing. This is talking about the end of the sales process a little out of order, but it works well because it explains where we will end up at the end of the training course: getting sales by different techniques.

After a break, the second half of the sales training is based on the steps of the sale, a well known concept that goes through introduction, questioning, features and benefits of your product, closing the sale, overcoming objections and closing again.

Winding up Day Two

The last part of day two is used to work on introductions, what to say and how, either on the telephone or face-to-face. Reviewing the day and setting homework around practising a sales introduction, a type of role play, for the next day and perhaps filling some forms out from the administration session usually works well.

Day Three

8.00 a.m.	Meet Franchisees for Breakfast
8.45 a.m.	Bring to Training Room
9.00 a.m.	Review Day Two
9.15 a.m.	Review Homework (Test)
9.30 a.m.	Insurance
10.00 a.m.	Administration (Stock)
10.30 a.m.	Coffee break
10.45 a.m.	Practical – Using products
12.30 p.m.	Buffet Lunch
1.30 p.m.	Introduction to Sales Part Three
2.45 p.m.	Coffee break
3.00 p.m.	Marketing Part Two
4.15 p.m.	Coffee break
4.30 p.m.	Round Up and Homework
4.45 p.m.	Drop Franchisees at the Hotel
Evening	Free Time for Franchisees

Breakfast number three of the week can impact on your waistline, which is why the fruit bowl is a good option on day three!

The review of the previous day can be light-hearted, with a practice session on sales introductions. Keeping this section light is a great way of calming franchisees' nerves. It doesn't matter if they mess it up now, and next week is the important bit.

After the review and mini role-plays, the first session of the day is the important albeit dull subject of insurance. The only time insurance is interesting is when you need to claim but it is important to explain the reasons for commercial insurance and vehicle insurance and the reason why a blanket policy for all franchisees benefits the collective.

The salient points for insurance are what the policy covers and who to contact in an emergency. Having the account manager there is a good way of showing the broker's commitment to providing the business with support.

No matter whether or not the business is a supply franchise, a specific session on the subject of stock and how to get it is important. Even if the section revolves around standard stationery supplies, marketing items or actual products, the important lesson is how much to hold, how long before it is required to reorder an item, and how it is delivered.

Practical sessions often receive the best reviews from franchisees at the end of a course, which is why a sprinkling of practical sessions every day will make the less interesting sessions flow more smoothly. The previous sales sessions covered the basic steps of the sale process and it would be fair to assume that this should suffice, but successful selling is very much about repetition and practice, hence a further session is needed to cover objections and how to prepare proposals using the templates included in the franchise pack.

Exploring marketing techniques in a second session is a good way to conclude the third day, which is a mix of business information and promotion of this exciting new business that the franchisee has bought into.

Winding up Day Three

After three days the course is over the halfway marker and the prospect of starting a new business is both real and within touching distance.

After setting what will be the final homework session of the week and dropping off the franchisees again, the third day is complete for the training manager.

Day Four

8.00 a.m.	Meet Franchisees for Breakfast
8.45 a.m.	Bring to Training Room
9.00 a.m.	Review Day Three
9.15 a.m.	Review Homework (Test)
9.30 a.m.	Operations Manual Review
10.30 a.m.	Coffee break
10.45 a.m.	Bringing Products/Service together
12.30 p.m.	Buffet Lunch
1.30 p.m.	Running your business – Finances
2.45 p.m.	Coffee break
3.00 p.m.	Running your business – Pricing
4.15 p.m.	Coffee break
4.30 p.m.	Round Up
4.45 p.m.	Drop Franchisees at the Hotel
Evening	Take Franchisees to Dinner

By now the flow of your course will be established in the minds of the franchisees, with a review every morning of the previous day and any homework set.

Day four is a perfect time to review the operation manual and bring together what the franchisees have learned during the week and how this learning fits into the manual that they will take with them in just over 24 hours. Reviewing the manual also provides you with an opportunity to answer any questions from the first three days' instruction.

The final session of the morning is a specific way to bring the products or services offered together in a relaxed manner. Combining the mix of products or services will give the franchisees a better idea of how they can maximise the potential of every customer they secure.

It is essential to teach franchisees the best way to control finances. The session just after lunch is a good time to explain finances and how important it is to understand proper financial control in a business. This is where a relaxed and basic approach works and instead of lots of facts and figures the best way to relate to franchisees is often a comparison with everyday life.

Use examples of home finances to illustrate how balancing the home bank account is exactly the same as running a business bank account. Once you have covered how to balance the bank account and franchisees feel more comfortable, you can then move onto other financial tasks required to control finances.

With the importance of finances covered, the next session links in nicely with the subject of pricing. There are plenty of franchises that allow franchisees to set different prices for the menu of products and prices. If your franchise fits into this category then demonstrating how a franchise can develop pricing policies will show the impact of lower pricing on profits. The important message is that holding out for optimum prices is the best way to work and that setting cheaper prices only devalues their business and essentially makes a franchisee work harder to achieve the same profit they would have made had they maintained the original prices.

Winding up Day Four

The final night in the hotel is the perfect time to entertain franchisees, take them for dinner and a few drinks and chat about positive things. Setting homework is a bad idea – give the franchisees a night off. There will be plenty to discuss in the morning after everyone has had the opportunity to delve into personal lives!

Day Five

8.00 a.m.	Meet Franchisees for Breakfast
8.45 a.m.	Check out from Hotel
9.00 a.m.	Bring to Training Room
9.15 a.m.	Review Day Four
9.30 a.m.	Vehicle Leases or Premises Review
10.30 a.m.	Coffee break
10.45 a.m.	Uniforms and Stock
11.15 a.m.	Bringing Sales Together

12.30 p.m.   Buffet Lunch
1.30 p.m.   Light-hearted Role Plays
2.45 p.m.   Coffee break
3.00 p.m.   Review of the Week
3.30 p.m.   Wave Franchisees off

The end of a long but fruitful week dawns on the final day with the final collection of the weary franchisees from the hotel. Breakfast might be a cup of coffee after the calorie hit from four previous breakfasts, or a cooked breakfast to soak up the previous night's consumption!

It's a good idea to stay in the same hotel so that you can retire without having to take a taxi home, only to rise and face a drive to the hotel - unless you live five minutes away that is.

The best format for achieving the aim of a highly motivational last day is a review of the week followed by a fun-filled day of activities.

Mobile styled franchises require the handover of the vehicle, which is where a session with the leasing company fits very well into the last morning. For premises-based franchises or home run operations, this session can be tailored to the planned set-up for their launch the following week.

There is nothing better than giving new franchisees a big box of goodies, such as uniforms, promotional items and even pens and literature. They're all part of the set-up pack that they have effectively paid for but it can still feel like Christmas to receive lots of new gadgets while psychologically it softens the gut-wrenching feeling after parting with the hefty cheque a few weeks before.

Notwithstanding the importance of administration, this function is redundant for any business without sales, and so the primary consideration for any training course is generation of turnover. Sales are the key to success and the focus of the final day, so that when you send your franchisees off into the wide world of business they are confident with the basics and ready to approach customers. This is where a review of sales techniques and the unique selling points of the products or services that your franchise offers is imperative. You must be confident that franchisees understand the sales process.

A session before lunch followed by some light-hearted role plays in the afternoon is the best way to confirm the transfer of knowledge from a week of training.

Role play is often seen as embarrassing and some franchisees freeze or cower in the corner if it is too serious, which is why it has to be light-hearted. Some franchisors use video cameras and analyse performance, which in my opinion is far too invasive and can create negativity. The alternative is to create some bizarre scenarios, and task the franchisees with a goal of gaining an order, finding out a piece of information, or getting commitment to a demonstration. A mixture of cold calls and appointments for the group not only provides the franchisees with a varied role play scenario but it is incredibly useful to others.

The best way is to have the group looking on while one franchisee sells to the trainer. The reason for this is simple. The trainer can help if the franchisee loses track with a reverse sale by saying something that helps the franchisee get back to the sales process. Don't forget that this is a motivational exercise, not a nit-picking assessment which will determine the future of an employee. If you need to help the franchisee during the role play then they will learn more from the group review afterwards if someone else suggests what they should have done.

The group review can take place after each role play scenario or at the end, when all franchisees have taken their turn.

During my time with ChemEx the role plays were fantastic fun and Gary Allard was a master of the wind-up role play, taking franchisees out to their mobile showroom and then unloading lots of products, passing them out to the rest of us who would walk off with the stock. The important message was that if the franchisee was not careful, stock and profit could simply walk away. I guarantee that all the franchisees took this lesson with them and although we all howled with laughter at the time they would never lose track of stock. Ever.

There were plenty of other scenarios and wind-up role plays but perhaps they are best kept out of this book and confined to the memories of those who were there.

Winding up the course

After this jovial session it is the perfect time to let the franchisees load their luggage and box of goodies before returning to the training room for one last time, this week at least.

After a week of learning and with some franchisees facing a long journey home, the final session is best kept brief and to the point.

It is always beneficial to get feedback from franchisees at the end of a course, a subject covered in more detail in the next section of the book. For now, asking franchisees to fill out a survey form often provides you with positive feedback and a piece of signed paper for their file.

Wrapping up a course is a transition from student to graduate and is the final opportunity to offer wise words of encouragement.

After thanking your new franchisees, bring your staff into the room or the foyer to personally wish every franchisee success before waving them off.

So there we have it: an induction training course example that contains lots of theory, a little practical application and some interactive sessions to build franchisees' confidence.

A great time to interview potential new franchisees is when a course is taking place, so that they see real people who have already decided to sign up. Another reason to make sure that your course is fun but fact filled!

What do you think? – Getting feedback to improve your course

I mentioned the survey questionnaire in the last section and indicated that this is a good tool for two reasons. First, you have a signed document that is a record of the training and if the course is good enough the comments should be positive. This signed form can really help you later if a franchisee happens to lose their way and starts to claim that they have not received training in an attempt to either get their investment back or to receive additional support.

The second benefit from the comments made on a post-course survey can help you refine the course for future franchisees. Comments made about individual sections indicate where improvements in training methods or training tools might enhance the experience for the franchisee.

The wording of the survey is also important. Try to keep the form simple by using marks out of ten instead of leaving gaps for comment. Leaving two boxes until the end for the franchisee to add a general comment and suggestions for improving the course is adequate.

A good idea is to have a final comment box with a direct question such as "what is your goal for the first year?" This normally generates a very positive response, which is useful when assessing each franchisee's motivation level.

Don't fall into the trap when asking for feedback, use tick boxes and ratings instead of asking for detailed analysis

Good luck – Sending franchisees out into business

The time lag between waving off the induction course and starting to trade should be the shortest possible.

The only time when a delayed start is acceptable is if the franchisee is waiting on completion of a lease for premises and the anticipated completion date falls between two courses. If this is the case then that franchisee is far better working in another franchisee's business than sitting at home waiting to start their own.

For the vast majority of franchisees the launch of their business will coincide with the end of the induction course and thereafter Monday morning is day one.

It is the responsibility of a franchisor to provide initial support in the new place of business, which means that on the first day someone is on the doorstep of the home based franchisee or at the premises as applicable, promptly at 9.00 a.m. This might involve someone from the support team staying overnight in a hotel to avoid a long journey first thing Monday morning.

The format for the day varies from franchise to franchise but the main objective is to start selling to people as soon as possible. This involves knocking on doors, delivering brochures or telemarketing.

There is often a team of support staff for larger franchise companies and although your new franchise may not have the resources as yet, it is important that if a premises launch requires input from you as the franchisor that this work is carried out during the induction training course so that your new franchisee can start trading right away. Sometimes this is not possible and the work required to "shop fit" premises is part of the post-induction course support.

Setting a store up may involve synchronising computers to the franchisor's mainframe or commissioning machinery, such as the large vinyl printers used in Signarama stores. This commissioning process is often done by the manufacturers, especially when the equipment is expensive and requires expert engineering skills. Once commissioned, the equipment should work properly and any problems must be resolved before the franchisee starts to use it.

It is important to try to get some business for your new franchisee on the first day or at least quote for business; if you can't show that it can be done then how can you expect a rookie to do it themselves?

Can I hold your hand? – Essential support in the early days

After the euphoria of an induction course and the pure adrenalin rush of launching their business, franchisees will still need support and guidance, much the same as toddlers need a parent to help them cross the road or learn to write, although the time scale from toddler to adolescent is accelerated in franchising terms.

The first few weeks are critical in achieving this aim, so set the benchmark for how much support you can commercially provide.

Franchisors, especially in new franchises, often make the mistake of providing too much support because they have very few franchisees to support. It is an easy mistake to make when you invest in a person to support the network, and that person appears to be redundant with so few franchisees to support. Although sending them out to offer more support appears to be the easiest option, it sets a precedent and in some cases can delay the independence that you need to instil in your franchisees.

It is far better to use the employee for other tasks and provide the agreed and contracted support.

The "hand-holding" period depends entirely on what this contracted support is. A day a week for ten, fifteen or more weeks, or two weeks then a day every week for a month; whatever it is try to stay focused and provide exactly what was agreed.

I am not saying that you must not offer additional support because I am fully aware that the difficulty comes when you are trying to establish a new franchise and the success of your venture depends on recruiting lots of franchisees, which is certainly helped by successful initial franchisees. The temptation is to over-compensate and get lots of business for them by offering lots of support, which contradicts the previous paragraph. This quandary is one that you must consider, but be careful if you do over-compensate because it may cost you dearly in the future if franchisees who join later expect the same support and success.

File it away

Keeping a record of the support days is essential and some franchises even have pre-printed stationery that has spaces for comments and signatures so that the hearsay problem is eradicated. The risk analysis part of this is that if every visit is documented and held on file then in the future if a franchisee cries "no help" you can refer to the signed documents and show that you have fulfilled your obligations.

Communication is the key to successful franchising and to assist the process it is a good idea to instigate internal file notes written by anyone dealing with a franchisee in a support role. By this I don't mean every phone call documented but if, for example, a franchisee has a problem with stock or delivery, a quick note in say the accounts programme, which is accessible for authorised users, makes sense. As the franchise grows and lots of file notes are written then a weekly circulation list for management works well, keeping the management team abreast of activity. There is nothing worse than a franchisee calling the Managing Director who originally sold the franchise about a festering concern and having the rant met with silence because nobody has given the MD a heads up.

Another tip is to use the time between the office and home to call franchisees from your hands-free kit!

Taking the dummy away – how to wean franchisees off daily visits

Supporting franchisees is one thing but running their business for them is another. If you spend too much time then the freedom and autonomy that they yearned for initially will diminish in their minds and they will probably resent the input.

Remember that you have given them a system to work to and an operations manual to refer to, which should provide all of the answers that they seek.

Weaning franchisees from daily support is a gradual process and involves a little planning.

The best way is to maintain daily contact with visits for one or two days in the first week and then phone in the morning and evening for the remainder of the first week. For the second week try one or two days field support and a call at the end of the day for the remainder of the week.

Spacing the calls out to one or two a week, with a day with area support, will help the franchisees develop independence and confidence to develop their business.

Your aim should be a field visit every four to six weeks after the first three months to review progress, while phoning once a week. If you use this philosophy then every support manager you employ will be able to look after 15-25 franchised units and still dedicate time for training courses and the launch of new franchisees.

Of course if a franchisee is really struggling you can provide additional support if you deem it appropriate at the time, but if you do offer this additional support the extra days should be noted and again added to the file for future reference.

I often found that regular support visits ended up as a wasted day riding shotgun or twiddling my thumbs if the franchisee did not have anything specific to do, such as a joint presentation to a big client. To combat this waste of resource it is a good idea to make sure that the franchisee planned a day full of activity in advance of any support visit. Carrying out regular business reviews is another good way to use the available time effectively.

It is impossible to provide you with a definitive guide of questions that franchisees ask but it is fair to say that in most cases the type of questions that get asked in the early stages revolve around products or services offered.

As time moves on these types of questions reduce as the franchisee learns their trade, at which point support usually changes to assistance with business development and growth. Your support team may embark on joint visits to regional accounts or help with a tender for a local authority, much the same as a salesperson would if employed on an area.

The occasional franchisee just isn't performing and their idea of support is for the franchisor to send someone to get orders for them to generate cash. This short-term fix placates the franchisee until the next visit, but watch out for this trap because more often than not the franchisee will wait for regular support and not strive to gain business themselves.

What is abundantly clear to me after many years in franchising is that after a year or so franchisees who have started to achieve good growth, and by definition have a successful business, start to question what benefit regular visits are at all. Yes it is true; they often see support as an intrusion and start to ask what other benefit they can achieve for the royalty fee charged.

Regional and National Accounts

One way round this is to divert the support team from working directly with the franchisee to working on regional or national accounts in the franchisee's area, which can add business for the franchisee and perhaps other neighbouring franchisees.

The danger here is failing to deliver results for the franchisee in a timeframe perceived as acceptable. Regional and national accounts take time to secure, which for an impatient franchisee is unacceptable unless they understand the process. In short, you must manage franchisees' expectations.

Although it is very tempting to provide more support than contracted for new franchisees, make sure that you don't create a precedent that future franchisees will expect.

16

You've Cracked It

Or so you Think!

Let's sit back and count the dough – If it was only that simple!

Everybody's happy – Communication with your growing network

Throughout the book I have mentioned that communication with franchisees is a fairly important component of running your network properly.

With any family discontent is occasionally evident, although you strive for harmony. Discontent often starts with a small niggling problem between family members that grows into a conflict because it is not discussed and the problem grows. The franchisor can avoid this problem by talking to their family regularly and find out if there are any niggling problems that they can work out before they grow into problems that perhaps could affect more franchisees.

When you operate a franchise company you must grow a thick skin and take a rational pragmatic approach to the rants of franchisees. Unfortunately, a text book cannot teach you to identify the real concerns.

The best advice is to address concerns quickly and develop dialogue by calling franchisees regularly to see how their business is developing. These regular conversations will provide feedback on a variety of subjects and enable you to identify concerns that could escalate. In many cases the feedback you receive provides you with an opportunity to explain and counter-argue a simple dispute before it gets out of hand.

Apart from file notes and feedback from franchisees, regular internal meetings with the support team to review the development of each individual franchisee is another good way of maintaining up-to-date knowledge about your network.

Talking to franchisees encourages positive communication that helps you create good success stories. Indeed, most of the communication process is positive and rewarding, unless you are running a poorly supported network.

The best way to conclude this section is to think of the network as a time-bomb with a clock that you control. The timer can be wound back but only when you speak to a franchisee. If the franchisee is content, then you are able to turn the dial back. This is not an option if you don't talk to a franchisee or they remain unhappy. To prevent the timer running out you need to keep the majority of franchisees happy so that you have enough opportunities to rewind the timer and keep the business safe.

Later in this chapter I have identified common concerns in the section that considers the best way to police a network.

Attempt to call franchisees regularly even if you have subordinates looking after the support function. A call from the boss shows that you care about your franchise partners.

RSVP – Regular regional meetings

Providing franchisees with regular updates through regional meetings is a proven way to ensure continuity in a franchise. I mentioned regional meetings from a franchisee's perspective in Chapter 7 and the same requirements apply for franchisors.

Regional meetings are a luxury when you have a larger network with franchisees located all over the country, as these take time. As a rough guide, a regional meeting should have at least four franchisees so if you have 20 or so then having four or five regional meetings works.

For a network of less than ten franchisees it is probably better to have one central meeting, which is the best option for new franchises in the first year or two.

The content of a meeting again depends on what your business provides through franchising. A product-based franchise should use the opportunity to launch a new or reformulated product so that attendees are aware of the changes, while a service-based franchise should concentrate on a new niche market or system process that has become available.

The format of the meeting will evolve over time but as a guide, half a day is usually sufficient to allow for transfer of information and general discussion.

There are plenty of conference suites available in hotels that are situated close to motorway junctions for easy access and although delegate rates vary it is possible to have a room with tea and coffee on tap and a few platters of sandwiches for a reasonable price.

Start early, but allow plenty of time for franchisees travelling from afar. The rule of thumb is that if someone has a two-hour journey to the venue then 9.00–9.30 a.m. is about right.

After the courteous welcome and introduction try to keep the sections short and motivational, with lots of positive points before moving to the discussion part of the meeting, often referred to as the "open forum".

The open forum is an opportunity to communicate in a group but it has the potential to become a kangaroo court if caution is not used. Keep control of the discussion by treating the meeting as a board meeting, with questions and comments directed through the chair, otherwise a melee could develop very quickly.

Although the open forum is essentially a moan session, it is an excellent way to bring out and discuss ideas and opinions on subjects that affect franchisees, while giving you the opportunity to diffuse problems immediately. As some points require investigation it is a good idea to take notes and respond to franchisees, individually or collectively, within minutes of the meeting.

I enjoyed regional meetings immensely and they were fun, even the ones with grumpy franchisees. If the support team knew that a particular meeting was going to be difficult we would prepare, with the team mixed in around the table so that we could keep eye contact instead of being side by side. This worked really well and I remember working with Gary Allard when we would play with the franchisees in some ways. Gary and I developed almost telepathic qualities which let us see what the other was thinking. We would let franchisees discuss to the point that they could almost touch a radical change, only to have a firm "no" at the perfect time. This fun was short-lived though, once the franchisees got wind of the wind-up, but it lasted a good thirty meetings.

Don't forget that the franchise agreement is fairly comprehensive and stipulates the franchisor's total control over fundamental changes. In 99% of points raised by franchisees you are not required to do anything at all, if the agreement was drafted properly.

At the end of the open forum it is also a good idea to introduce some positive feeling, which is achieved by a round-table discussion on the subject of success stories.

Feed your attendees before they go back to their businesses and make sure that you mingle and thank everyone personally for taking time to attend.

National meetings and conventions

National meetings are an excellent way to get franchisees together for an informative day, or series of days, with social events breaking up the serious side of the communication process.

You don't have to have a grand event with gimmicks at extreme cost, so perhaps for the first one a day meeting with lunch is the best option. Keep a similar format to the regional meetings, albeit with more content and possibly a keynote speaker talking success in their personal or business life and the uncanny resemblance to your plans for the future and how the franchise, with excellent franchisees, is going to achieve the target.

Delegates should have a bag of goodies with sales literature, promotional items and samples of new products if they are available. A nice touch is a motivational book such as "Who Moved My Cheese" by Dr Spencer Johnson. A wonderful parable that reinforces the message that people need to branch out and find other places where their "cheese" is, instead of getting their "cheese" from the same places all the time. The "cheese" is whatever they seek in life and therefore those who "seek" what they want will have more chance of finding it than those who wait for what they want to come to them or be found in the same old places they frequent. It is a great book and takes only about an hour to read but the message stays with the reader for a lifetime.

Planning a bigger event requires a lot of input from the team and even external help from audio-visual companies and venue advisors to ensure a smooth and well presented meeting. It is not unusual to expect franchisees to pay for accommodation and contribute towards the overall cost; however this can mean that some franchisees miss the event because of the cost factor.

The bigger the event the greater the cost and time needed to prepare, rehearse and entice franchisee delegates. It can take months of planning for a few hours of presentation, but with a fantastic effect on sales for a short time because franchisees leave motivated and hungry for success.

Some franchisors combine trade shows with the convention, with key suppliers paying for space to display their wares and a chance to sell new equipment or services. This contribution offsets the overall cost and can reduce the investment for the franchisor or franchisees.

A gala dinner with entertainment and awards for franchisees is a superb way to end an event of this magnitude.

Before I scare you to death, it is prudent to mention that conferences or conventions don't have to happen every year and even the larger established franchises only have them every two years or so.

Regional meetings show your commitment to communication and the desire to listen and learn from franchisees who are on the front line of your business.

Just visiting – Meeting for a coffee at short notice

There is nothing better than calling in to a franchisee's premises or home while you are out and about. If the franchisee operates a mobile business then a call to see what part of the area they are working in and then an offer to buy them a coffee also works.

Some might see this as invasive, but I disagree for a very good reason. Individual franchisees are using your name and image under licence so why not visit unannounced to see how the premises or van look?

Apart from the spot-check scenario it is nice to say hello without any agenda at all.

Meeting with senior franchisees for lunch or dinner is beneficial, especially if you want to maintain harmony in a franchise. Senior franchisees help develop systems and usually work the system properly, so they are excellent role models for new franchisees. They also help in regional meetings when a rookie franchisee goes off at a tangent and gets pulled back into line by the senior franchisee as opposed to the franchisor; this is a very powerful message when it happens and a massive vote of confidence for the franchisor.

Make sure that you are visual to franchisees not stuck in an ivory tower. Meet for a coffee or a bite to eat and take an interest in their business, it the least you can do for the faith they had when they signed up.

Hello, hello, hello – Policing the network

You have a franchise agreement which clearly states the acceptable parameters, so why do you need to police the network at all? Well, probably for the same reason that every state has law enforcement; some people fracture the occasional rule, regulation or law.

Don't be naïve when you set up a franchise and assume that everyone is adhering to the contract to the letter. Thankfully most do, and use open forum discussions to present alternative ways of operating or suggesting a different supplier. There are some, though, who will risk the wrath of the franchisor to save a few pennies.

It can start over the price of a toilet roll when a franchisee finds a similar product for a few pence cheaper and then questions the price charged by the franchisor. If the franchisor doesn't address the question and fails to justify the price of the toilet roll, its superior quality and the importance of every franchisee selling the same product to protect brand and product association, in time the unanswered question grows into a problem and a revolution, over a few pennies.

This is the first way to police the network, through communication. Unfortunately just "talking" is never enough in isolation and at some stage policing a franchise requires the enforcement of the "power of audit" clause. This clause is a definite requirement in the franchise agreement, with clear parameters for entering and inspecting storage facilities or records without prior notice.

You are nicked!

There have been plenty of occasions when a dawn raid carried out by a team of support managers has resembled something like an SAS operation. Often referred to as "Operation Baseball Bat", the aim was to shock franchisees and show that we, as the franchisor's team, were serious about breaches in the agreement. We always used the cover story that we carried out the dawn raids because we were protecting franchisees that were playing by the rules. Thankfully most audits that I have been involved in raised only a few irregularities that required a rap on the franchisee's knuckles, similar to a warning issued to an employee for lateness, for example.

When you consider audits you have to be prepared to enforce the clauses that were breached if a franchisee has been very naughty. In plain English this means you must terminate a franchisee's agreement if the breaches are blatant and considerable, using the employment analogy of being similar to gross misconduct.

Believe me when I say that I have not taken any pleasure out of terminating any of the naughty franchisees I have had the displeasure of encountering. Well perhaps one or two, especially the one who shrugged off a previous warning and foolishly bragged about the fact that they would continue no matter what. That termination ended acrimoniously and the former franchisee in question lost his territory, any value and faced a hefty bill when he attempted to fight the termination. Indeed, he ended up owing more money to the franchise for loss of income. That sunny day spent inside a solicitor's office proved to be long but satisfying.

For the most part I have taken solace in the fact that the franchise networks that I worked with have understood the reasons and supported any termination. Surprisingly, sales increased after any audits. Funny, that!

Resist the temptation to become a tyrant! Work with the network rather than dictate.

Therapy helps – The overall psychology of franchising

It is very easy to over-complicate everything, analyse to the extreme and role play every eventuality when operating a franchise company.

Indeed this book might have been less than a hundred pages if I had decided to make it more of a rigid "how to" without some analysis or reasoning.

Much the same as running any business, there are days when customers or employees pose a problem and as a manager of people you must address any concern and nurture the customer or member of staff so that the business moves on. The difference is that in franchising you are responsible for the franchisees and this increases the number of concerns or problems that you face every day. Some days are quiet and others appear to be nothing but days of solving problems that require diplomatic intervention.

Maintaining a balanced management approach takes practice, lots of practice, and it is not unusual to feel consumed by negativity if niggling little problems require more and more of your time.

If you think that running a franchised business is a 9–5 job, think again! Franchisees will contact you just as a meal is placed in front of you or you pick up the car keys to go out. You can decide not to answer a call but I guarantee the problem will manifest itself over night and be ten times worse in the morning, so my advice is to take the call and placate the franchisee, even if you say you will investigate it the next day. Unfortunately plenty of franchisors don't possess the leadership qualities that franchising needs and this is probably the reason that they don't have a happy network. I am a great believer in people taking vacation time to unwind and relax. This philosophy extends to everyone, including the principal of the business. Wait a minute. Perhaps I should take my own advice – no, too much child-maintenance to pay!

Seriously, there is one sure way to lose sight of targets and goals and that is to immerse oneself in the business and work in the business rather than working on the business. Time management, as mentioned previously, is an essential skill-set for all tiers of the business structure and even the principal must take time for himself so that he can work effectively. The principal needs time to step back from the mundane tasks to see the periphery and recognise areas that need attention or tasks that need monitoring.

Rookie franchisors would do well to utilise the services of the consultant after launch, although most franchise consultants offer limited post-launch support. People avoid mentoring, which to me is madness, especially for a fledgling franchise in the first year or two. If the consultant has run franchise businesses then why not have them there a day a month or on the end of a phone as a business crutch? Agreeing a fixed non-executive fee, or a combination of equity at eventual exit and a reduced fee, is surely the best way to proceed.

Over time most people toughen up in the franchise world and develop skills that maintain balance in a business but some only develop limited skills, for which the only option is therapy! The good thing is that therapy does not equate to a session with a psychiatrist, although I have often said that franchise consultants need some skills in this area.

Running a franchise company isn't a massive headache; on the contrary, it is incredibly rewarding and exciting if the principal and subordinates accept that franchisees are a breed apart and need lots of love and attention, with a sprinkle of discipline and a side order of understanding.

Accept that running a franchised business is completely different from running a company-owned operation and that you need to develop additional skills to manage people employed as well as franchisees who probably think they own part of you for the fee charged to buy into your franchise. If in doubt, use a mentor to guide you through the transition.

17

We are Good at This

Growing, Developing and Exiting

This time next year Rodney – We will be millionaires!

Recognition required – going for independent accreditation

Well here we are, some way along the journey that started with an idea to expand a business and develop a concept in the world of franchising.

After recruiting new franchisees and running the business for a while you really have become a franchisor. Congratulations for now but there are a few things that you can still do to improve the image of the business and show the world that you are an ethical organisation.

Most countries have an association or independent organisation that oversees ethical franchising in their particular region. I referred to the directory of franchise associations available at www.franchiseassociations.org in the first part of this book. It provides links to specific franchise associations by country, a very useful tool if you are reading this book but are not a UK based company.

Each country also has legislation that is relevant to business operation but rarely has specific laws on franchising. Although this may change over time it is often better to have general legislation that captures all eventualities for every business.

Contract law is a very important part of licensing, with strict legislation on acceptable clauses and fair terms, which in some cases has precedent relative to franchising that has influenced franchise agreements over the last few decades.

This is where the relevant bodies, such as the British Franchise Association or bfa, provide franchise operators with acceptable parameters or "codes of conduct" that self-govern the industry.

Let me join!

If you wish to follow an ethical approach then adopting the codes of conduct as part of the operation is the first step. After a year or so, applying for membership is a positive move that can help with recruitment for the simple reason that a potential franchisee perceives your business as an ethical company.

The reason I have stipulated a year as a reasonable time period is that this provides the accreditation manager at the bfa with a track record to analyse. I am sure this is the same for other associations around the world.

The process is fairly standard, with a review of the franchise agreement and system as well as feedback by way of telephone interview and surveys with franchisees. There is analysis of the financial information for the business and this includes an appraisal of the fees charged and utilisation of those fees to help develop a franchisee. This is important as it is an unwritten law that franchisors use fees to develop the business for the benefit of all, not to siphon off fees for pure profit. It is recognised that franchisors should benefit from ongoing income from licence fees and product margin so that they benefit from franchisees' success, not from initial fees alone.

Accreditation is awarded to successful applicants and most are awarded associate membership, converting to full membership later.

Once achieved, bfa membership has the added benefit of access to a number of web portals such as www.whichfranchise. com and negates the need to complete a temporary accreditation if you want to exhibit at the main franchise shows.

The fees charged for membership and accreditation may change as this book sits on a shelf, therefore for an up-to-date price contact the association in your country or for the UK the bfa direct or visit the web site www.thebfa.org

In my opinion every franchisor should be a member of the bfa and even new franchisees should have an interim membership to make sure that they are following the codes of conduct right from the launch date; however with membership voluntary this mandatory ideal is a pipe dream for the moment. Perhaps in a few years I will have to revise this section, fingers crossed.

Accreditation and membership for most of the associations around the world is voluntary but your support and compliance is a very strong message to people looking at joining your merry band.

Sowing your seeds in next door's field – Exporting the concept

People get very excited when their little business flourishes and franchisees appear to be crawling over themselves to buy an area.

The euphoria continues until someone in a board meeting experiences an epiphany and shouts "let's hit America!" That three-word sentence is often the catalyst for potential world dominance, in everyone's imagination. The image of a Bentley Continental soft top parked outside a mansion in California, an apartment overlooking Central Park in New York and cruising from franchisee to franchisee in a Hummer along the I4 in Florida, is a hard one to ignore. All from that three-word sentence.

Plenty of clients and companies that I have worked for have considered exporting their concept. Some have achieved this but the field is usually closer with Europe, a more fertile option than the distant field with a "Stars and Stripes" on the gate.

Exporting a concept to the USA is not impossible but many have tried and failed while spending hundreds of thousands of pounds on promotion, legal costs and compliance costs.

This seems a tad unfair, especially with such a receptive franchise market in the US, given that plenty of concepts have arrived in Europe in the last fifty years.

Why, you may wonder? There is no definite reason apart from the fact that setting up in the US is like setting up 50 UK operations. Each state has a specific market opportunity with legislative requirements that can differ dramatically from Arkansas to Wisconsin.

The golden nugget is that if you do crack the US market then potentially 50 plus goldmines, each with a seam of Au as long as the Potomac River, is the potential reward.

One, Two, click, you are back in the room, eyes transfixed on the pages seeking the answer. Sorry to disappoint but there is no simple formula and if there was do you honestly think that I would write it in a book that sells for less than £15? Oh no. I would be driving that Bentley out of a gated mansion to the country club for a game of golf with Tiger or some other celebrity, vying for some inspirational insight.

With so much potential in the UK anyway, why not expand this first? And while you do, throw a handful of seeds into next door's ploughed furrows.

Stars and Stripes later – First Euro Stars

The first thing to consider is whether your concept fits another country at all, after considering cultural differences and demand. We are back to the analysis of the market, covered previously, but as an example if your business is say a car paintwork repair then every country has cars, so it is a massive tick in the box. However, if it is a franchise that responds to a need for electrical testing that was born out of specific UK legislation, then it may struggle in many European countries if the laws differ.

Thankfully, most concepts are transferable to the main European countries in our unified community but it is not unusual to find a similar franchise already working. People travel to franchise shows all over the world and copy franchise concepts. Being the first in a country to offer XYZ is still attractive to entrepreneurs, even if the concept is a loose hybrid version of a successful business.

What do I do then?

You can do your research from the comfort of your office or home, using the internet to find what franchises are available in a selection of target countries.

If you prefer, a consultant can investigate for you while you work on the home-grown franchise. Commissioning a brief report to find out what countries your franchise could fit is the first step towards spending a lot of money promoting the franchise.

Apart from the essential market information that a report or your own research provides, the key question is what benefit you can derive from selling a master franchise licence. In truth, a master franchisee is a bigger version of a local franchisee, with a higher price tag for the agreement and in turn higher set-up costs.

Signing a master franchisee is great for the profit line in the first year but unless they are the right individual the ongoing income can fall short of expectations, especially if the concept is a new idea in that country. Masters need to sell territories to build a network, exactly the same as you did initially. From that they need to recoup their investment through product margin or services rendered and in most cases you will take a slice of territory sales and of those products or services.

Buying the rights to a country for say £250,000 may sound fantastic but if this means a master needs to sell 20 franchises to recover £12,500 net profit it usually means at least a two or three-year programme and the ongoing running costs. For you the income might only be a fixed fee of £1,000 per franchisee, as an example, with minimal royalties, so the second and third years could mean an income of £20,000 to £30,000 in total.

This is where the potential is the key factor for a master or for you as the brand owner. If say you have developed fifty franchisees over three years then a conservative estimate is for a master to achieve 20–30 over the same period. On the other hand, if you have hundreds of franchisees then a similar proportion is a good assumption.

Selling is "a numbers game", no matter what you provide for the end user. It is no different for a franchise company. If you see enough people in a market that has a large demand and you offer a great product or service at value, then your chances of success are improved.

Much the same as you developed a great story for franchisees in your own country you need an international story with justification and analysis of the potential for each country available.

Researching the demographics and gaining an understanding of a country is essential preparation. This takes time to collate but may mean the difference between success and failure in the future.

What are the costs involved?

How long is a piece of string? You can spend a fortune on legal agreements if you are not careful before someone has sniffed at your concept and so I usually advise that clients get a quote for an enforceable contract, under the laws of a particular country or countries, as a guide. This can run into tens of thousands of pounds for each territory if lawyers based in the UK have to collaborate with a franchise lawyer in another country, and pay them in their own currency. Writing this agreement is essential and when a master fee of hundreds of thousands is at stake it is a calculated risk for you as the brand owner. The negative is that you may spend this vast amount in protection of your business and the potential master may not even sign up, therefore commissioning an agreement although time sensitive is usual after "heads of agreement" are in place. These "heads" will require some legal input, albeit at a lower fee than a fully blown agreement.

Trade mark costs are considerable for each country and often run to many thousands of pounds, with the additional associated timescale required to register and overcome objections from established corporations in individual countries or territories, assuming that your logo or name is similar.

Translating literature is another cost and is normally covered by the main business although it can wait until the agreement is in place. Providing a turnkey operation adapted for the country or territory being secured is a standard condition and therefore by definition the literature written in the mother tongue of the country is part of that provision. Using the master to help can reduce the cost but budgeting say £5,000 for translation and printing is normal.

A franchise that provides a product can mean that product approval and testing are required and regulations differ from country to country. These costs are again usually covered by the franchisor although occasionally the master is responsible. Find out if your product requires certification long before you get to heads of agreement. I remember in a past life a particular situation when the supply of each product meant a fee of around 1,500 Euros and with twenty core products much debate ensued over who paid the 30,000 Euros. In fairness, other countries did not have similar strict compliance even though products were certificated in the UK, a bizarre situation in this unified Europe! It was a stealth tax but no matter how much harrumphing took place the master could not trade without it.

Training, stock and support for the first two years are much easier to calculate and form part of the overall potential set-up cost, which is just the same as every franchise signed up at home.

Although this isn't a definitive costing you should expect to invest anything from £40,000 to £70,000 for every master franchise signed up.

This doesn't include any commission that an agent may charge as an intermediary in helping you secure an interested overseas franchise partner. This leads rather nicely into a section on getting someone interested so that you are in a position to offer the rights to that person or people.

Is anyone out there?

The good news is that people are continually looking to import concepts like your business so the normal recruitment process and advertising in magazines or on the net will bring regular enquiries to your inbox. Many master franchisees have bought the rights to a country after visiting exhibitions with no preconceived idea of what they wanted.

There are options to promote your business as an exportable concept on the various web portals and magazines. This flag waving approach is the norm for most companies and is attractive because it keeps the process internal, with enquiries driving initial contact and eventually agreement.

Buying and selling businesses is an industry itself, which uses overseas agents, trade commissions and independent advisors to place buyers and sellers together and instigate a deal. An offshoot of this is the buying and selling of franchise concepts via these sources, in addition to the wealth of experience offered by associations such as the bfa. A number of franchise consultants actively seek international investors on behalf of franchisors that want to expand to a particular region of the world.

Recruitment in general is very much down to circumstances and relies on someone looking for a business in a given area. If the area is available and the concept is attractive then the chances of success improve. This is where the PR and marketing are so important for home-based franchise recruitment and when you want to expand internationally.

Contact the bfa or your franchise consultant for help and advice initially and thereafter consider the best option for your business.

International partners certainly enhance the image of your franchise but make sure that the benefit is not limited to a pin on a globe. If you are serious about developing abroad then make sure the master ranchisee is committed to developing your brand.

Don't forget to tell everyone –
Maintaining momentum with PR

The first rule of PR is "any story is a good story – no matter what the content."

You cannot control how someone perceives an article, press release or advertisement. You might intend to write an interesting article but people will read words and sentences and then interpret, judge and derive their own opinions. You will never impress everyone who reads about your business and so long as you accept this your aim should be to write something that will appeal to the majority.

Business people often work in the business, not on the business, as I have already said on numerous occasions. With franchising especially you have to work on the business continually, adapting systems to cater for changes in products, services and markets if you intend to maintain a happy network of franchisees. Linked to this is the requirement to attract new franchisees to purchase vacant areas or to replace current franchisees looking to sell their business. In previous chapters I stressed the importance of working with franchisees and communicating so that new and interesting stories become easier to write and at this stage of the guide it is very important to reiterate this point.

The process does become easier as the network grows, with more opportunities to create viable examples of the success achieved by a number of franchisees.

Consider that people can take months if not years to make that decision about buying a franchise and during that time they perhaps read a dozen or more issues of a magazine or even case studies on a web portal. If you don't write new copy regularly and simply rely on old success to sell franchises, then there is a possibility that your business will appear boring.

New stories and new success will feed the desire for those keeping a keen eye on your franchise as a potential partner. A continual flow of new material also shows anyone that your business is evolving and growing. In short, they'll see that your franchise is exciting and vibrant.

Established franchisors often use a PR agency to have a dedicated creative individual write articles based on stories the franchisor obtained from regular contact with franchisees, and information the agency obtains in a follow-up contact with the franchisee. This may seem a little intrusive and a gain for the franchisor with nothing for the franchisee and so it is a great idea to get the PR agency to write a second article that the franchisee can use locally. Offering assistance in promoting the article in a local newspaper is an additional benefit for the franchisee as it helps them to promote the products or services available and generate more business.

Even if you decide to write and distribute articles without a PR agency, try to create two versions of the same story.

The core subject matter for any story is the message of success, growth, innovation and benefit for a customer using your business. The problem is that everyone selling franchises is doing the same thing, writing articles about the explosive success of their business! If everyone is doing well how can someone decide? The answer is that although I said everyone is doing the same thing, the reality is that very few are updating web portals or sending press releases or submitting copy for magazines.

Franchisors become lethargic and bored with PR, especially when everything appears to be going well. They have lots of people interested and because it takes time to sign franchisee up they don't notice the downturn in enquiries. The affect is lower recruitment three or six months later, all because the leads slowed down months earlier. Without mentioning any names, for obvious legal reasons, I have seen the dramatic impact on two businesses that I have had contact with in the past. The first example is a business that used to have lots of PR even though they were established and had a healthy network, in numbers at least. Even today, web portals have stories that I wrote or contributed to over three years ago, being careful here, with very little added since. Needless to say the network has decreased by over 25% since my contact. It doesn't take a genius to see that policy, as well as stagnant PR, has contributed to the loss of numbers and surely turnover and profit. Notwithstanding the possibility that a management decision to reduce numbers may be part of the strategic planning, in my opinion the image of success has vanished.

The second example is another established company that has increased PR activity in recent years and maintained a healthy churn of new franchisees, maintained network size and used the PR to recruit new international master franchisees as well. The basic management style is no different for either example, as both companies are run by experienced franchise executives, but the focus and realisation of the importance of maintaining fresh stories as part of the overall promotion of the brand is abundantly clear.

The important message here is to maintain the PR activity even when it appears to be a pointless task. Find stories to write

Keep the PR momentum and constantly reinvent quality stories to present the reader with a great image of your business!

from good things going on, no matter how insignificant they appear. Create news by working with franchisees – and a customer is the final message.

What about another one? – Using your experience to buy or set up another franchise.

It may seem like madness, but with all your experiences just think how much easier it would be if you set another franchise up.

Oh no, I hear you say! But think about it for a second at least. With another gem of an idea that complements what you already do, the set-up costs would be minimal and, with operating costs initially absorbed by the incumbent team, the risk is minimal.

Plenty of multi-brand franchise operators have made this decision. Minute Man Press, set up by Roy Titus, backed his son Ray who founded Signarama in the 1980s. To date, the United Franchise Group has a number of franchise brands that have evolved from pilot operations and acquisition of fledgling franchises, including EmbroidMe, Billboard Connection and Plan Ahead Events.

Closer to home, Castle Estates set up Calbarrie with much success and Chips Away launched Professional Car Cleaning, now Autosheen PCC, before selling the franchise to Farecla.

Diverse franchise brands work in multi-brand franchise groups, even if the separate brands do not appear to complement each other, because potential franchisees who don't have the finance available or interest for franchise A may be better suited to franchise B or C. A good recruitment manager can cross-fertilise and secure a sale, instead of losing a sale.

Importing a franchise concept is another way of multi-brand franchising, securing the master rights from overseas and developing a market while enjoying the security of a thriving franchise business to take the pressure off.

There are plenty of established franchise owners looking to sell for the right price. It is quite easy to spread the word in the franchise community if someone wants everyone to know. If handled properly and you make it known that you are interested in a good acquisition, opportunities will eventuate. Franchise exhibitions are notorious for loose-lipped individuals speaking to all and sundry about the invisible 'for sale' sign above the stand.

The good thing is that many of the franchises operating in the UK are concepts run by the founder or owned by a small group of private stakeholders, therefore negotiations are easier compared to the need for shareholders' meetings to consider an offer.

I am sure that the teenies and twenties will see more multi-franchise brands evolve globally and some very large groups will capture the attention of prospective franchisees.

Setting up a second or third franchise is a good way to use combined resource and offer franchisees choice within the same four walls. If franchises complement each other then referral opportunities and increased sales turnover for each brand can dramatically increase group turnover – and exit value for you!

Time to reap the rewards – Superb franchise for sale, silly offers accepted!

Passing the family business on to the next generation is an extremely unlikely occurrence nowadays and will probably become even rarer in the future. Privately owned businesses of any note are snapped up by conglomerates while the children of business owners now have opportunities to "find themselves" and opt for higher education and opportunities far afield in this shrinking planet. The idea of working for one's parent is simply not attractive any more to the majority of younger people.

The dynamics of business have changed in the last thirty years, with profitable businesses that can derive an income immediately attractive to individuals who have made very good money in previous employment. Raising the funds to buy an existing business is far easier today, with the equity in houses generated by the housing price boom over the last twenty years. Banks still lend, despite the crash, global recession and the impact banks and financial institutions experienced in the last decade. This is one of the reasons why franchising has flourished; people buy into franchise concepts to provide an income and small independent businesses are snapped up instead of being passed on to the next generation.

Venture Capital companies back thousands of investments with one eye on today but the other firmly on an exit and return on the funds provided two or three years later. Buying and selling businesses over short periods for investment profit is not unusual and has made plenty of people very wealthy, but adopting this quick build and rapid sale has contributed to the demise of the business that is generated, maintained and family owned for decades.

Businesses are always for sale, even if there isn't a sign outside the building. If someone approaches an owner and makes the right offer then temptation is very hard to resist.

All very interesting – But what about my business?

Approximately 80% of clients want to know what type of return they can expect if the exit in two to five years. This common question is absolutely right and for the remaining 20% I broach the subject anyway. Planning an exit, or even a target value, is very much part of proper strategic planning so that investors know the potential, based on what a business with similar turnover and profit would sell for now. Realising a substantial value at exit depends on a well run, tight and transparent operation with fairly contented franchisees and regular income streams and cash flow. This is why it is so important to set the business up with a standard franchise agreement for every franchisee and excellent administration to avoid irregularities that may affect the value when someone carries out due diligence as part of a possible purchase.

Every franchise business is different but it is fair to say the ones that have international potential and yet more prime areas available in the home country secure a future-value bonus if the potential is real and achievable.

Decision made – time to sell

Positioning your business for a sale is a big project and requires a lot of thought and careful timing.

We all wake up occasionally and stare at the alarm clock, hoping it is three hours fast, but deciding enough is enough based on one bad day is irrational.

If you have followed a course mapped out by a strategic plan then positioning the business for sale is probably part of that plan, albeit often slightly out of kilter with the original planned exit process. It may possibly be on achieving a particular number of franchisees or a certain turnover figure, it matters not what the trigger is as long as the margins are in line with the plan or profit projections made some time ago.

Stability and growth are the key factors that a buyer considers when looking at the purchase of a business, particularly a franchised business, therefore you must position the business accordingly. Erratic turnover and inconsistent recruitment will present the buyer with a difficult decision: whether to make an offer at all.

This is why, despite the temptation to milk the situation and secure fees before a new owner takes over, it makes good sense to position the business for sale at a time when new franchisees are due to start or there are plenty of enquiries. If the negotiation is handled properly you can secure a higher price anyway, and so the benefit is still there.

How much then?

The most important question for 99% of people is, how much then? It is the same for franchisees and every business and is a number plucked out of the air with a million added to the spurious figure.

The answer is the same as stated in the other half of the book; it is how much someone is prepared to pay, and thereafter whether this is acceptable. No, really!

I have recently supported a client looking to acquire an established but poorly run franchise. The vendor wanted a substantial price for the franchise but the accounts showed that this was ten times the net profit declared. My opinion, for what it is worth, was to state that the vendor was having delusions of grandeur or something, resembling a long necked spotted animal found in the safari park. The vendor's rationale was the future potential and despite my aching sides the client was prepared to pay the figure, and so the deal progressed. Being the consummate professional that I am, getting the new business to a level that makes the agreed price insignificant is the focus, and time will tell, but if the profit and growth match the belief of the clients in question then the exit value could make the purchase price insignificant in the future. Of course if they had managed to secure it for half the price that potential would be better, but what do I know!

As a rule of thumb, if you want to sell a business for seven figures, in this day and age, it really needs to have a net profit of at least £200,000 on a good day. Five times net profit is achievable but usually with some excellent future potential. For a turnover-based sale, two to three times turnover is exceptional and reliant on the margin differential.

Future value, similar to the example above, is the dragon's den approach, which is now a favourable way for people to value franchise businesses as long as they have a sound rationale for the potential growth or income stream improvement through national and international expansion.

As things could change dramatically, the best advice is to ask your accountant, who will have a better idea of valuations at that time. This impartial view is the basis of setting an achievable value and clearly highlights the acceptable parameters of the negotiation phase later.

With the business positioned for a sale it is time to polish the windows and prepare for a deluge of interested buyers. Remember to remain focused and run the day-to-day operation though.

For sale or not for sale, that is the question

As principal or one of the owners putting a business on the market, maintain decorum and confidentiality, especially with employees and franchisees. Obviously some key people need to know at the right time but news of a pending sale often causes concern and creates an unstable business.

Over and over again people advertise firms for sale only to find that the competitors capitalise, or in the case of franchise organisations franchisees stop paying licence fees because of the uncertainty. This is where advertising or broadcasting the "for sale" status is potentially dangerous and needs careful planning. If you do advertise your business then keep the initial details ambiguous and keep the name off the advertisement. Use a post office box or an intermediary, such as a consultant, to filter any responses.

It is highly likely that any sale will not come from a printed advertisement anyway and so confidentiality is maintained. It is more likely that a business agent will act for you, seeking out potential buyers from their clients' enquiries. Alternatively, a business agent can approach potential buyers to present an opportunity, only disclosing salient information after a non-disclosure agreement is in place.

Sorting the wheat from the chaff

When you sell your house you get nosey people in and it's just the same for businesses being sold. Unscrupulous people looking for a quick deal and fast buck from a business sale are common. They assume that you are desperate to sell and look to usurp your little empire for a ridiculous price in the hope that you will snatch their hand off. Show them the door unless you are looking for a quick "fire sale".

Not that any buyer will try to acquire the business for a better price, but if you are determined and believe the valuation is fair, then holding out is the obvious call.

It is exactly the same as selling a franchise to a franchisee; believe in the commodity and sell the features and benefits, this time on a collective scale as the whole package. Enthuse about the fantastic opportunity to grow and deliver excellent profit, coupled with the realisation that you have other goals and ambitions.

Of course you might wish to stay on for a period as part of the sale agreement, which is a good option if you want to secure a payout whilst keeping some involvement, and it often suits an investor to have a handover period in place to preserve stability for franchisees as well.

Whatever you personal agenda, make sure that you understand the implications of selling your business and the tax liability, especially with a complex system for capital gain tax and relevant relief, which may or may not apply depending on legislation at the time. Your accountant is the best person to ask about the real cash value of any future sale. You may consider an offer of £2m fantastic and more than enough to retire on, but this is going to be far less in cash terms after the government nibbles a slice of the figure.

Once more, and for the last time in this book, the complexity of selling a business is a subject that could fill a book, if not a volume of books, if I were to cover all eventualities.

The important message and a final piece of advice is to first make the franchise work: deliver profits and an acceptable personal income for the shareholders. Selling the business is a pension and realisation of the efforts that you have made over the life of your business under your tenure and is the icing on the cake.

What you will do with that pension is pure fiction at the moment and I wish you success, whether you retire or move on to another business or invest in the next big thing.

Before I leave you to build that empire

We are all passengers on the journey of life and this book is part of mine: a legacy that may stay hidden in the annals of time, a book alongside other reference guides, surpassed by new ideas and thinking. Or maybe it will be considered by some as something useful and enlightening that helped them on their own journey.

If one person nods in approval then I have fulfilled my intention and the hours of work have been worthwhile.

Thank you for reading, and good luck on your journey.

per ferreus opus nos planto nostrum own fortuna
(with hard work we make our own luck)

Part Three
Acknowledgements & Suggested further reading

Very special thanks to Alan Guinn for sharing his knowledge, without any reservation, and for suggestions and comments that make the book far better than I dreamt of.

www.alanguinn.com   www.theguinnconsultancygroup.com

Special thanks to Lee E Hargrave for not only his kind permis-sion to refer to his own published work but for the inspiration and guidance offered personally.

Plan for Profitability – How to Write a Strategic Business Plan by Lee E Hargrave

Published by Four Season Publishers is available from Amazon ISBN 1-891929-19-4

How to Get Control of Your Life and Time by Alan Lakein

Permission granted as per the copyright notice as the reference made is a review.

Published by Penguin Books available from Amazon ISBN 0-451-16772-4

Thanks to the following publishers for their kind permission to mention the following books;

Who Moved My Cheese by Dr Spencer Johnson

Published by Vermillion, Random House Group available from Amazon ISBN 0-09-181-697-1

Other Books by Chris Gibson (updated 2013)
So...You Want To Buy a Franchise? by Chris Gibson and Alan Guinn © 2012
Advice on buying a franchise - with anecdotes and advice for US and UK franchisees
Parent Print ISBN 978-0-957618-4-2
ePub ISBN 978-0-9567618-3-5
Mobi ISBN 978-0-9567618-2-8
Selling - It's Not A Mind Trick by Chris Gibson and Alan Guinn © 2012
Sales techniques explained from cold-calling to running sales teams from the CEO's chair!
Parent Print ISBN 978-0-9567618-5-9
ePub ISBN 978-0-9567618-7-3
Mobi ISBN 978-0-9567618-6-6
Fifty Shades of Nagging - Most of Them Grey! by Chris Gibson © 2012
A satirical look at relationships and what men refer to as 'nagging'
Parent Print ISBN 978-1-909429-00-0
ePub ISBN 978-1-909429-01-7
Mobi ISBN 978-1-909429-02-4

Special thanks to the Jim Rohn International for allowing me to convey a very important life message stated by Jim Rohn – a wonderful motivational speaker sadly missed.

www.jimrohn.com

Special thanks to Franchise World – Bob and Nick Riding – for the belief in the writings of a young man!

www.franchiseworld.co.uk

Thanks to Mark Scott – Director with Nat West/RBS Franchise Department – for your candid views and comments prior to publishing.

Finally very special thanks to Rushmore Editing Services for a fabulous job converting waffle into selective prose.

www.rushmore.edu

Useful links – The following web sites mentioned in the book

www.alliebooks.co.uk
www.franology.co.uk
Franchise World   www.franchiseworld.co.uk
Photography and Design   www.iheartstudios.com
Domain Registration   www.123-reg.co.uk
The British Franchise Association   www.thebfa.org Franchise
Associations (list)   www.franchiseassociations.org Wikipedia
www.wikipedia.com
www.direct.gov.uk
Franchise Finance ww.franchisefinance.ltd.uk
Which Franchise   www.whichfranchise.com
Franchise Direct   www.franchisedirect.co.uk
Franchise Gator   www.franchisegator.co.uk
Franchise Magazine   www.franchisemagazine.net Franchise
Development Services   www.fdsfranchise.com Making Money Magazine
www.makingmoney.co.uk
What Franchise   www.whatfranchisemagazine.co.uk Executives Online
www.executivesonline.com

Printed in Great Britain
by Amazon